Praise for *The Cards*

"When life hands you lemons, pick up *The Cards You're Dealt: How to Deal when Life Gets Real* by Theresa Reed. With unabashed humor, truth, and compassion, Theresa tackles tough questions that tarot readers often face, such as how to handle health readings or help those experiencing grief. She provides guidance on what to say to those who may be suffering, scared, or overwhelmed. As any tarot reader worth their salt knows, the way you deliver a reading and the connection you build with the person are just as important as the accuracy of your tarot card interpretations. Theresa Reed's expertise makes her the perfect guide for your tarot journey, offering deep healing insights from a place of authenticity and truth. Drawing from her years of experience as a professional reader, Theresa generously shares her own life stories, making this book not just about reading tarot cards but also about fostering empathy for both yourself and others. It's an invaluable resource for learning how to read your tarot deck when you are most apt to draw cards the most: at crossroads moments that eventually come for all of us."

—Jenna Matlin, author of *Will You Give Me a Reading?*

"Not everything in life is easy and often when people seek out a tarot reading it's because they are experiencing something difficult. This is one (of many) reasons why Theresa Reed's book, *The Cards You're Dealt* is essential reading—both for those who read tarot professionally and for those who wish to seek out a reading in order to address a tough situation. Theresa pulls no punches in this work as she guides the reader in a gentle and supportive way into unlocking the meanings and medicines that the tarot can provide when we experience hard stuff. Reed is not only an amazing reader herself, she is also someone, as she shares in the book, who personally navigated tough situations throughout most of her life, making her a truly exceptional guide."

—Briana Saussy, author of *Making Magic* and *Star Child*

"Theresa Reed has written the exact book I need exactly when I needed it. *The Cards You're Dealt: How to Deal when Life Gets Real* is a deep (and deeply personal) dive into the confusing and often isolating world of loss and grief. Far from the 'love and light' gloss of pop spirituality, Reed takes us through the blood and guts of mourning so we can lead ourselves and our tarot clients to the glory of acceptance and healing. Her guidance on how to communicate with grieving people is beautifully stated and universally useful. The dictionary of card meanings and collection of spreads are accompanied by examples, exercises, and tips that make this book accessible to novices and experts alike. Theresa Reed is an incredibly kind and wise soul, and this book reflects that perfectly."

—Melinda Lee Holm, author of *Your Tarot Guide*

"*The Cards You're Dealt: How to Deal when Life Gets Real* is another wonderfully needed creation from Theresa Reed. We all deal with the things life throws at us, and many times we seek out our trusty tarot readers for advice, support, or just to create a plan to help us navigate these often tricky situations. In this book, Theresa gives practical and easy-to-use advice to make your readings the best they can be when dealing with death, dying, or being a caregiver. The journaling and activities included also help you, as the reader, process the emotions that come up for you if you are navigating these situations as well. With each tarot card broken down with meanings and card spreads, you will have the confidence and guidance you need to become a more in-depth tarot reader and understand the depth of emotions facing end-of-life situations and how everyone reacts differently. Theresa shares examples and her own experiences to help you create a practice surrounding these topics to guide others and better understand yourself. I highly recommend this book to anyone who wants a better understanding of human nature when faced with the prospect of death and its many facets, whether you are a beginner or an experienced reader.

—Jen Sankey, author of *Magickal Manifesting with the Moon*, *Enchanted Forest Felines Tarot*, and *Stardust Wanderer Tarot*

"Theresa Reed has never been a tarot reader that shies away from the hard questions. It is a completely admirable trait and one that I have always wondered how to cultivate it in my tarot practice. In this book, *The Cards You're Dealt*, Theresa shows us exactly how to do that: look at the hard topics and be willing to read tarot on them with an unflinching but compassionate gaze . . . and always in service to the sitter. Through practice exercises, pro tips, and tarot spreads on job loss, global tragedies, and grief in all its forms, Theresa has indeed written a book that is not typical in its treatment of the taboo subjects that most tarot readers would rather avoid. Confront them we must, if we are to be well-rounded readers, and to serve our sitters in times they need us most. This book is a necessity for any professional tarot reader."

—Hilary Parry Haggerty, author of *How to Read Tarot*

"*The Cards You're Dealt* is not a 'love and light' book that glosses over the shadows of death and grief. It's a compassionate, practical, step-by-step guide to how we can truly learn to heal and help others heal. The stories that Theresa shares are vulnerable and real, sprinkled with her Scorpio Moon humor. This book is for both tarot beginners and seasoned practitioners. You will want to come back to this book over and over again—it is filled with so much wisdom and magic."

—Pamela Chen, author of *Enchanted Crystal Magic* and *Tarot of the Owls*

"Theresa Reed is such a blessing. She has given readers a gift with this book by providing practical, real-world advice that's as encouraging and engaging as it is informative. It's a must-read for tarot beginners and enthusiasts alike."

—Mecca Woods, astrologer and author of *Astrology For Happiness and Success*

"In *The Cards You're Dealt: How to Deal when Life Gets Real,* Theresa Reed presents a transformative tarot guide that bravely delves deeper than the surface, shedding light on life's intricate challenges and the truths they reveal. Rejecting spiritual bypassing, Reed's voice—rich with decades of experience and genuine understanding—emerges as a beacon, guiding readers to confront their rawest moments with authenticity, courage, and unparalleled wisdom. Each page reveals Reed's deep expertise, showcasing tarot as an invaluable ally in healing, clarity, and life-navigation. As she explores the shadows of loss, illness, and complex relationships, it becomes clear that Reed isn't just an author; she's a luminary in the contemporary tarot landscape. Whether you're a seasoned enthusiast or a tarot newcomer, this book is not merely a guide. It's a revelation, a compass, empowering its readers to navigate life's tumultuous waters with unmatched grace, resilience, and purpose."

—Mat Auryn, bestselling author of *Psychic Witch*

The CARDS
YOU'RE
DEALT

The CARDS YOU'RE DEALT

How to Deal *when* Life Gets Real

A TAROT GUIDEBOOK

THERESA REED

WEISER BOOKS

This edition first published in 2023 by Weiser Books, an imprint of
Red Wheel/Weiser, LLC
With offices at:
65 Parker Street, Suite 7
Newburyport, MA 01950
www.redwheelweiser.com

ISBN: 978-1-57863-803-1

Library of Congress Cataloging-in-Publication Data
Names: Reed, Theresa (Tarot reader), author.
Title: The cards you're dealt : how to deal when life gets real / Theresa Reed, the Tarot Lady.
Description: Newburyport, MA : Weiser Books, 2023. | Summary: "A tarot guide that's not about predicting the future but about dealing with and healing from the tough stuff we all face every day: loss, illness, challenging relationships"
– Provided by publisher.
Identifiers: LCCN 2023017549 | ISBN 9781578638031 (trade paperback) | ISBN   9781633413030 (ebook)
Subjects: LCSH: Tarot. | BISAC: BODY, MIND & SPIRIT / Divination / Tarot | BODY, MIND & SPIRIT / Inspiration & Personal
Growth Classification: LCC BF1879.T2 R439 2023 | DDC 133.3/2424--dc23/eng/20230623
LC record available at https://lccn.loc.gov/2023017549

Cover and interior design by Sky Peck Design
Interior images from The Weiser Tarot © Red Wheel/Weiser. Used by permission.
Typeset in Candara

Printed in the United States of America
IBI

10 9   8 7 6 5 4 3 2 1

For Terry,
may our time here be long and our lives well lived

For Rachel Pollack,
who taught me so much. Your legacy will continue to inspire.

Please note

Tarot is *never* a substitute for therapy, grief counseling, legal advice, health-care advice, or other professional services. While it can be a help on your journey, it's important to be wise and consult licensed experts instead of relying on what the cards might say.

CONTENTS

PART ONE

Tarot 101   3

PART TWO

Spreads for Guidance   97

PREFACE:
THE DEATH CARDS

No one here gets out alive.

—JIM MORRISON

MANY YEARS AGO, on a hot summer day, an elderly woman came to my office for a reading. She was tiny and frail but somehow managed to lug her oxygen tank up the stairs. Her granddaughter was with her and could have helped, and I offered as well, but she insisted on doing it herself.

After situating herself on one of the worn vintage chairs, she took a few minutes to catch her breath. It's not easy to do when you can't get your air . . . and the weather is muggy. Once she began to breathe a little easier, she looked at me with those unforgettable steel-gray eyes and said, "I'm dying. I want to use this reading to make sure everyone will be okay after I'm gone."

We carefully moved through every relationship that concerned her. She was especially nosy about the granddaughter who sat quietly on the couch, glancing up infrequently as she busied herself scrolling her phone. There were tears and laughter as we covered everyone who mattered. In the end, she looked relieved. "Well, now I know I can go in peace." She smiled, paid me, and that was the first and last time I saw her.

In my long career, this was one of my favorite readings.

I will admit that I'm actually quite comfortable with this topic. The reason might be that death and grief have been constant themes in my life since I was young. That's not surprising when you learn my mother came from a family of thirteen and my father from nine. With odds like this, it's pretty likely you'll be going to many funerals in your lifetime.

My mother was also a sickly woman, which meant my childhood prepared me well for caretaking. Early on, I was expected to help because she couldn't manage all on her own. Her bouts with illness landed her in the hospital so often that it seemed like her second home.

Years later, when she passed away suddenly, I was left in charge of my ninety-something-year-old father. We had a challenging relationship, but I was the only one he trusted to handle his affairs. I can assure you that this job was no easy feat.

Not only did our personalities clash, but Mom had left him with a mountain of debt, and there were no funeral plans in place. To top this off, a few quarrelsome relatives decided to make this journey a miserable one, with constant drama and sabotage.

These were the most depressing four years of my life. But I had no time to feel sorry for myself. I had to get Dad to the finish line with grace—while running two businesses and caring for my children, who recently lost their father. Self-care became a distant memory, so having a glass or two of wine was the only way to wind down at the end of my long days.

I had support during this period, but the one ally that helped me move through this time was Tarot. Every morning, I turned over a card for reflection. From time to time, I would pull out the same spreads I used with my clients whose situations mirrored mine (oddly, it seemed as if I was surrounded by grieving clients with similar stories at this time). I created new spreads to help them . . . and these helped me.

My father was a strong man until the end. Dad smoked and drank every day, but his body hung on until it couldn't. He moved in with my brother in the last year of his life. My house was out of the question due to the steep stairs (plus, Dad hated my cooking, which was "too fancy" for his tastes). Having company made his days less lonely, even though he missed his independence.

One day, he fell and bruised the back of his head. After a short stint in the hospital, he came home and went straight to bed. This wasn't odd for him, so we weren't too concerned. The following day, my sister-in-law said he was still asleep but would be getting a home visit from a hospice nurse. The hospital had insisted we start working with hospice due to his advanced age. When the nurse came in, she quickly assessed that he was actively dying.

I immediately canceled work and headed out for the sixty-minute trek to see him. As I walked into the room, Dad looked up at me and said he was glad I was there. Then he said, "I think God is coming to take me."

"Are you okay with that?" I asked.

"I just want this to be over" was his reply.

Over the next few days, the hospice nurse checked in while various family members and friends came by to say their goodbyes. Dad was in and out of consciousness, so no one was sure if he was aware they were there.

On the last day, my sister-in-law said he was out of it. I came into the room and said hello. He immediately reached up, grabbed my hand firmly, and then let it go. I could tell he felt safe now that I was there. Again, I'm the one person he trusted, even though he despised my culinary skills.

I sat by his bedside, keeping vigil, occasionally leaving the room to talk to my younger brother or the hospice nurse about arrangements. I anointed his forehead and quietly sang songs and recited prayers. The hours came and went. So did the hospice nurses and a few more visitors. Then, finally, one of our relatives, a nurse, stayed with him for a few minutes and announced he would be "hanging around for days." My sister-in-law and I thought that was a strange thing to say, but this relative was the nurse, and what did we know?

After this relative left, we decided it might be best if I went home and returned in the morning because it was getting late. So I walked over to the bed and said, "I'm going to leave now, Dad. I'll be back tomorrow. It's time for you to get this show on the road and go to the light now." I turned around to get my coat, looked back, and realized he was dying.

I called in the family members who were left, and we stood around him, holding hands as he took his last breath. Once that happened, my sister-in-law looked up at me and said, "He always needed you to tell him what to do."

We laughed over that and then got busy wrangling all the details so he could have the funeral he wanted and deserved. There was no drama, no negativity. Just people coming together to help their father get to the other side with peace, comfort, and dignity. Then it was time to grieve.

Years of caregiving didn't allow me the space to process my feelings about my mother's death, which meant I had a lot of stuff to work through. But, once again, Tarot helped me navigate this tender time like an old friend who understood exactly what I needed, especially when I didn't.

One day, I decided to do my Mediumship spread to see how Dad was doing. As I laid down the cards, I was struck by the joy present. But when I turned over the last one,

I gasped. It was the Queen of Wands, the significator for my mother, a fiery Sagittarius. This card was a sign he was with her. I burst into tears and finally felt the grief I needed to acknowledge. Not just for the loss of him but also for her. Tarot was helping me heal.

It's funny because many people assume the Tarot is a scary thing. Popular media promotes this stereotype with images of women swathed in scarves pulling the Death card and exclaiming physical death is imminent. No matter how many times I explain that the Death card has nothing to do with dying, people still worry about it showing up during a reading.

Our culture also has a fear-based view of dying and grief. As Megan Devine says in her book, *It's OK That You're Not OK*: "The way we deal with grief in our culture is broken." We treat it like it's a pile of dirty clothes that needs to be laundered and put away as swiftly as possible. Often, we offer up useless platitudes such as "he's in a better place" or "everything happens for a reason," which sweeps feelings under the rug. Those statements are actually a way for those who are not grieving to push their own uncomfortable emotions away. We don't know how to grieve or to help others cope. We just want the discomfort to go away. It's the same with topics such as illness or caregiving. Instead of listening and offering the right kind of support, we call people "saints" and "brave" while we quickly look for an exit.

Imagine if we could face illness, death, caretaking, and grief with courage and compassion. Think about how different the energy would be if there were love and acceptance instead of fear. Tarot can help turn these tender topics into a meaningful way to connect and mend hearts. I'm proof it can help in the healing process, and I have seen it bring closure to many of my clients.

No matter whether you're facing an ailment or struggling to let go of a loved one, Tarot listens.

In this book, you'll learn how to work with the cards to find a solace no matter what cards you've been dealt. I can assure you this isn't a sad book, even though our topic may be. It's also not centered on "toxic positivity," the tendency to dismiss negative emotions with a forced (and fake) state of optimism. Instead, this book is about healing as we move through death, grief, and caregiving.

Of course, life has many other challenges we have to navigate. Divorce, the empty nest, aging, and more. These experiences can be difficult, but we can find grace even in the thorniest circumstances. I've helped clients ride these choppy waters, and I've also had to learn to swim with those currents. I'm sharing some stories, helpful Tarot spreads, and advice in the "Navigating Life's Hard Passages" section. When we face the hard stuff with courage, we can transcend the chaos and discover peace, no matter what.

I hope this book gives you the support you need so you can live well when life seems to be handing you all the hard cards. Because ultimately, that's it: when you are present in the now, loving your life as you care deeply for others and peaceful with the terms of your own mortality, that is really living.

May we all find our way with love, compassion, and awareness.

xo

Theresa

INTRODUCTION: WHY?

I HAVE WANTED TO WRITE this book for a long time. Partly because I couldn't find anything on the topic. But also, I have done the work with Tarot on myself and my clients. So many of the people I've read for over the years were coming to me for help with these delicate situations. Because illness, death, caregiving, and mourning have played such significant roles in my life, I'm also intimately familiar with them. I know the feelings, the hard truths, and the misunderstandings that come with this territory all too well.

I'm also quite comfortable talking about tough topics. It might be my Scorpio Moon or the fact that I find these topics more compelling for Tarot readings rather than the standard "Will I get married?" type queries. I like the hard stuff. That is where I shine and do my best work.

As I said before, the topic is heavy, but this book is full of hope. There is no trying to cover the shadow with "love and light." Instead, this is a practical book with readings and practices to examine feelings and experiences around death, dying, illness, caregiving, and life passages through the lens of the Tarot. These are topics we will all deal with at some point in our lives. This book is balm for the soul when you're overwhelmed and need to find solace, healing, and compassion for yourself or others. Like the Hermit's lamp, it's a small light during the times when you cannot see.

How to Use This Book

We'll start out with a brief intro to the Tarot. This way, if you're new to the cards, you'll have a basic understanding. Next, we'll go through each card in the deck with possible interpretations for our topic.

I'll cover each topic with stories, journaling prompts, Tarot spreads, practices, rituals, and exercises. They will help you deepen your connection to the cards—and find what you need to begin the healing process. I'm also adding pro tips for professional readers so you can show up in the best, healthiest way for your clients.

Feel free to go through this book at your own speed. Put it aside when you need a break. Pick it up again when you want to. Go over the exercises as often as you feel called, and try out the spreads that speak to your situation. Highlight what stands out, fill in the blanks, and add your notes in the margins. Do not be too precious or careful. Healing is not an easy or neat practice, and this book is meant to be used.

I'd also recommend having a favorite deck, pen, and journal. Journaling is my favorite practice for working through grief, sadness, and loss. It's a sacred space to jot down your feelings, Tarot spreads, and revelations. Your journal is a trusted companion on this journey. Pick one you love and make time to write in it. Daily practice is great. But if you're not feeling up to it, that's okay. It will always be there for you when you're ready.

Let's begin our journey with a solid introduction to Tarot.

PART ONE

TAROT 101

THE BASICS

B EFORE WE BEGIN WORKING with the Tarot, it's wise to start with a proper introduction. Whether you're new to the cards or a seasoned pro, understanding the basics will give you a solid foundation. Having this foundation is essential if you want helpful, accurate information.

A Little History

No one is quite sure where Tarot began. There are many myths and theories, but the oldest decks can be traced back to Italy in the 1400s. Back then, they were rare and expensive. They were hand-painted, which meant only the wealthy could afford them. For example, the oldest known decks, the Visconti-Sforza Tarot cards, were commissioned by Filippo Maria Visconti and Francesco Sforza. There are no known complete sets of this deck. Currently, they are scattered in museums around the world.

In the early days, Tarot was played as a trick-taking game known as "Trionfi" or "Trumps." It is still played in many parts of the world. However, the cards became associated with divination when Jean-Baptiste Alliette (also known as Etteilla) published a book in the 1700s. This publication gave Tarot a big bump in popularity with the public; now it's known more for predicting the future.

Tarot became more popular when the mystic A. E. Waite hired the artist Pamela Colman Smith to create the Rider Waite Tarot (now called the Rider Waite Smith, or RWS, Tarot). This classic deck inspired most of the modern cards you'll see on the market today. The beauty of the RWS lies in Colman Smith's rich art, which contains symbols and archetypes for each card. Also, unlike many other decks, the "pips" are illustrated, making them easier to interpret.

Over the years, Tarot became mainstream. As a result, the cards are often featured in popular culture. In fact, fashion designers have used the cards as inspiration for clothing and perfume!

Tarot has also evolved with the times. No longer just a tool for prophecy, it is used by modern readers for creativity, therapy, and storytelling. As Tarot's popularity continues to grow, who knows what new uses people will find for it? The sky is truly the limit for this ancient oracle/game!

Buying Your First Tarot Deck

You might already have a deck or two. (If you're like me, you may have hundreds!) But if you are new to the cards, you may not have one yet. Thankfully, we live in a day and age when you can easily procure one. Local bookstores or metaphysical shops usually have an excellent selection; plus, the internet opens up possibilities for every sort of deck you could imagine!

It's essential to take your time when making a decision. Once again, the internet comes in handy. You can explore different decks, including indie-published ones. What appeals to you? Cats? Modern figures? A deck with representation? A *Star Wars* theme? You'll find them all!

But if you can't decide, you may want to grab a copy of the Rider Waite Smith Tarot or the Weiser Tarot. They are classics and never go out of style!

If you've heard a rumor that someone else must purchase your first deck for you, that's not true. I think it's best to pick your own instead. That way, you ensure you're getting a deck you'll love and use often. After all, no one knows your taste better than you.

Once you have chosen your deck, it's time to "season" it. Seasoning means establishing a connection to your cards. My preferred method is to simply spend time with your Tarot cards every day and shuffle them as much as possible. Sitting in front of the television with your favorite series is a perfect time. The more you do this, the stronger your connection will be.

You may also choose to bless the deck. Blessing could mean saying a simple prayer or invocation over the cards or putting them in a window under the moonlight. Some folks like to pass their Tarot cards through sacred smoke. Others sleep with the deck under their pillow. Whatever works for you is all that matters.

You can store your deck in a wooden box, special bag, or silk scarf when not in use. I keep my most rare decks stored in their boxes in a cabinet. My workhorse deck remains out in the open for easy access—but safely away from anything that can spill on it!

Over time, you may decide to purchase more decks. You may even have different ones for specific purposes. For example, a deck with soft colors for healing work or an animal-themed one for the younger folks who want a reading. You'll have no trouble finding many cool ones to add to your collection!

Tarot Apps

Some people prefer Tarot apps over cards. I find this alternative to be acceptable, especially if you have trouble shuffling the cards. Apps can be just as accurate. Don't assume one is better than the other. The intention of the user is ultimately what matters.

What's Inside the Deck?

There are seventy-eight cards in a traditional Tarot deck. Newer decks sometimes include extra cards, which can add additional interpretations. Still, you don't need anything more than the basic seventy-eight.

Tarot is divided into two main sections:

The Major Arcana

The Minor Arcana

The Major Arcana represent fate, major themes, important lessons, the soul's journey, and the bigger picture. It's the stuff we cannot control, but it helps us grow.

The Minor Arcana are associated with day-to-day events such as work, finances, conflicts, and relationships. These are the things we can control to some degree.

Within the Minor Arcana, you'll find four suits, similar to playing cards. Those suits are the Wands, Cups, Swords, and Pentacles. Each suit has a set of themes connected with daily life.

Wands: work, passion, enterprise, action, Fire element

Cups: emotions, relationships, intuition, Water element

Swords: thoughts, conflict, stress, Air element

Pentacles: money, values, possessions, Earth element

The Minor Arcana also contain four figures in each suit called *Court cards.* They represent people in your life or attributes you currently express (or need to). Based on the Court member, they can also indicate messages, actions, nurturing, and mastery. They're tricky to interpret, but with time, you'll begin to see which role they play.

Pages: young people, students, messages, new beginnings

Knights: young people who identify as male, actions

Queens: mature people who identify as female, nurturing or creating

Kings: mature people who identify as male, leaders, mastery or completion

Myths and Misconceptions

I would be remiss if I didn't discuss some common (and wrong) stories you may have heard about Tarot. So here are a few myths we can dispel once and for all:

Your first deck needs to be gifted. I've already mentioned how important it is for you to choose your own Tarot cards. This superstition is totally bogus and a surefire way to ensure you get a deck you don't like . . . or never receive one at all.

Tarot is evil or the work of the devil. Sigh. Some folks feel frightened by the imagery. Others have been told by their religious leaders that the Tarot is bad. Still, popular media will portray the cards as cursed and readers as shriveled old hags or sexy, mysterious vamps raising their eyebrows in fear as they proclaim all sorts of maladies and danger. Tarot is simply seventy-eight paper cards. On their own, they are neutral. Like any tool, the user decides if they are for healing or nefarious uses. Also: anything can be used for good or ill. Period.

The Death card means I am going to die! Nope. Ironic to say this in a book about illness and death, but the Death card is associated with transformation. Despite the fearsome image, this card has little to do with crossing over. Can it ever mean death? Yes. But predicting the end isn't simple. Interestingly, I've found that the end-of-life readings are usually happy cards like the Sun. I'll speak more of this later in the book.

You must be psychic to read the Tarot. I'm a firm believer that everyone possesses intuitive abilities. However, some folks trust their feelings more than others, which may create an illusion that they are "gifted." If you start paying attention to your hunches, you might find you're right on more often than not. Tarot is the perfect tool to strengthen your connection to your higher guidance!

No one should touch your cards. This is a matter of preference. Some Tarot readers want the querent to shuffle their cards, whereas others don't. Those who don't want you to touch their cards view them as an extension of their self and spiritual practice. Ultimately, the choice is up to you. Frankly, I prefer people not to touch my deck because I've had many a deck destroyed from sticky fingers or aggressive shufflers.

You need to know all of the meanings before you begin. That's not true. While having a solid foundation in traditional interpretations is good, you don't need to memorize anything before reading the cards. The cards provide visual cues, just like a picture book.

You must learn reversals. I admit I was once guilty of this idea myself. I assumed you'd need upside-down cards to deliver a solid reading. Lo and behold, I had a few readings with folks who didn't use them . . . and they were accurate. Once again, this is preference. Try them out, but if you're not feeling it, you can choose to ignore them.

Tarot is always accurate. Well, I like to say the cards are always right, but human interpretation can be faulty, especially when you're invested in the outcome. For example, if you only want to see a certain thing, you'll find it. Say you're asking about lost love and want to know if they'll return. You pull the Three of Swords, a card of separation. This card could cause anxiety, or you may ignore it altogether and come up with something that makes no sense to the card you pulled but satisfies your desire. This is why you need to be grounded—something I'll speak about soon.

Those are some of the most common misconceptions about the Tarot. I hope I've dispelled them properly. Now let's move on to how to do a reading.

How to Do a Reading

Doing a reading is straightforward. You come up with a question, shuffle the cards, pick one (or more, which is called a *spread*), look at the images, and start talking about what's going on in the card(s).

While that may seem like an overly simplified explanation, it's true. Tarot reading, at its heart, is not complicated or only for the special few. In fact, I like to say readings are very much like "picture books," the first books we encounter as children, which help us to learn how to read before we understand letters and numbers.

When you approach the Tarot from that perspective, you'll see it speaks a language through symbols, archetypes, and art. Think of how you feel when you notice certain symbols in your life. For example, a stop sign tells you to stop your car. It's a universal image we all know and understand. In Tarot, you'll also see certain things that relate to your daily life.

For example, looking at the figure in the Eight of Pentacles, you'll see someone hammering away on a golden pentacle. Right away, you know this has something to do with work or fixing things. Simple, no?

Reading the cards doesn't have to be any more complicated than that. Here are a few prompts to help you begin reading with confidence:

1. Look at the picture. What's going on? Begin describing the scenario.

2. If there are figures on the card, how are they interacting . . . or not? What conversations might they be having?

3. Is there something in the image that catches your eye? If so, pay attention and use that for interpretation. For example, the butterfly crown on the Queen of Swords might suggest a metamorphosis.

4. If you are working with more than one card, look at them like a storyboard. What is unfolding?

5. How are the colors making you feel?

6. If you were one of the figures in the card, which one would you be? And what might you have to say?

7. Are there any symbols that make you curious? If so, why?

8. If you feel uncertain, you can consult a book. You might use this one or the little white book that came with your deck. It's okay to refer to a book! Even seasoned pros will whip out a trusted book when they are stumped!

These are simple techniques, but they work.

With practice, your readings will become fluid. Soon, you'll see how the traditional meanings stack up with your perceptions. Finally, you'll find your "Tarot voice" and make the cards uniquely your own. Remember: no Tarot reader sounds the same, and there is no one way to read the cards. Ultimately, you'll discover what works for you over time.

Exercise: Let's test this out right now! Grab your Tarot deck and begin shuffling while you focus on a question. When you feel ready, put the deck facedown, cut it into three piles, and put it back together again. Pull one card off the top of the deck. Use the eight prompts in this chapter to begin interpreting. For example, if you draw the Three of Cups, you might describe it as a party among friends (prompt one). Perhaps these folks are celebrating exciting news or partying down after a long work week (prompt two). Keep going . . . and watch your interpretation unfold!

Words to the Wise

If you're coming to the reading with an attitude of dread or feeling overly attached to a particular outcome you want, the reading can be skewed. Also, if you're impaired (or if the other party is), interpreting what's in front of you could be challenging.

It's always best to approach Tarot readings when sober and open to the wisdom the cards want to deliver.

A simple grounding practice before you begin will help you create the right mindset for the work. I like to do a short meditation or simple breathwork. A few minutes of quiet introspection or prayer can help set the right tone.

Some folks like to recite a little invocation before they begin, such as "May these cards connect with my higher guidance and help me see the truth I need to see most today." Feel free to create your own!

Here's my favorite grounding practice.

Belly Breathing

Belly breathing is the easiest way to "get in your body." I use this practice all the time, not just for Tarot readings! Here's why: when life is handing us a bucket of lemons, it's tempting to check out. Even when you're not a fan of what's happening, being present allows you to experience life fully. Instead of worrying about the future or ruminating about the past, you're simply here, now.

Being present is also important for Tarot reading. After all, it's mighty hard to find the message in the cards if you're distracted. Being present allows you to drill down and see the story unfolding.

Breathwork and meditation are helpful tools for grounding. I'll mention a few more practices throughout this book, but let's start with belly breathing.

Here's what you do: begin inhaling deeply through your nostrils. Next, take the breath down into your belly as if you are inflating a beach ball inside it. As you exhale, gently pull your stomach in as you press the air out while you visualize the beach ball deflating. Keep your breath slow and steady. Soon, you'll notice a calm settling over you. Now you're ready to read Tarot (or do whatever). That's it.

Do this practice before reading Tarot. Do it when you're in the middle of a reading and feel scattered. If you're reading for someone else, do it together. Syncing your breath is magical! Lastly, engage in belly breathing whenever you feel stressed, sad, or out of sorts.

Some Tarot Dos and Don'ts

While I'd like to say that the Tarot has no rules, there are a few things to keep in mind as you read. These things apply to beginners and pros alike.

The first: do take your time. Do not rush the process, especially if dipping into sensitive territory. Instead, give the cards time to "breathe" by carefully examining each one.

Do use Tarot as a tool to compare options and make better decisions. Tarot readings often lead to valuable insights that help create intelligent, courageous choices. Life is a series of decisions. Knowing what's up puts you in the driver's seat.

Do use Tarot to connect with your intuition and confirm your hunches. Tarot is a remarkable tool for accessing your own inner wisdom. The answers are within you; consider Tarot your key for unlocking those answers. The more you work with Tarot, the more you'll trust your gut.

Do use Tarot for a quick hit of guidance or inspiration when needed. I keep a Tarot deck with me at all times. You never know when you might need some mystical support!

Do use Tarot to connect with something greater than yourself, whether you call this Spirit, the Divine, Universe, God, or some other term. Tarot is a spiritual tool . . . and a fantastic way to strengthen your connection to your higher guidance.

Do not worry about being wrong or right. This desire will create rigidity or trepidation in your readings. There will always be times when you see clearly and other times when the messages are murky. Do your best. Treat every misinterpretation as a lesson rather than a mistake. Go easy on yourself.

If you're reading for others, listen more than you speak, especially when approaching tender topics. You may feel compelled to deliver information, which is fine, but often Tarot is more about a dialogue instead of a one-way conversation. Allow space for the other person to talk, give feedback, ask questions, and cry.

Avoid giving fatalistic readings. I mean that you don't want to say, "This will definitely happen" or "This won't happen." Instead, look at the possibilities as well as detours and new perspectives. Plus: the future can always change. We have the agency to turn things around at any time.

If you don't like the outcome, resist the urge to repeat the reading. A clarifying card is fine, but constantly hammering the same question will only lead to frustration. By that same token, you'll also want to refrain from allowing other people to do that with you. For example, I once read for a woman obsessed over an ex. Every other question was about whether he would return to her. She even tried to cleverly word further questions to skew the interpretation to the outcome she wanted. Tarot doesn't like that. My cards started getting snarky, and she was soon getting mixed messages.

If you're reading for someone who seems to be struggling, be sure to have a list of helpful resources nearby. Therapists, counselors, and other healers might be necessary depending on the situation. As I mentioned before, you do not want Tarot to take the place of a licensed professional.

Some readings may get uncomfortable, especially those centered around the subject of this book. When that happens, it's okay to take a break. Go outside, grab a cup of tea, and leave the reading to simmer for a while. If you feel triggered, putting the cards aside for a spell is okay. You can always revisit the topic when you feel up to it. Keep in mind that if you're reading for others, there may be times when you touch on something, and that leads to a strong reaction. Create a safe space so they can express their feelings without fear, shame, or blame.

You'll also want to be careful about platitudes such as "It's for the best" or "It is what it is." Statements like that are rarely helpful and often diminish the other person's feelings. They can also create an "ending" to the topic and cut off the ability to go deeper. Platitudes are often a way for the person who said it to end the subject because they don't like where it's going!

Sometimes people are not ready to hear what the cards want to say. That's okay. Give any information you have and let it go. They may look back on the reading later and feel differently about it. Or maybe they won't. Again: this is okay. Do not take it personally. (Psst, follow this advice if you don't dig what Tarot reveals to you.)

Do not use Tarot as a substitute for professional medical care. You'll also want to avoid turning to the cards for legal or psychological advice. Leave these questions for licensed practitioners.

Do not use the Tarot to predict death or illness. It doesn't work like that . . . and you certainly don't want to inject fear into people or yourself. While Tarot can show energy around these topics, it's never guaranteed, and it's not that easy to predict those types of things. We'll talk about that in upcoming sections.

Tarot is not a mind-reading tool. Asking about what someone is thinking isn't productive for the Tarot. Frankly, I find it's best to ask someone directly instead of using Tarot as your spy tool. The same goes when asking questions that are none of your business. While there is nothing wrong with seeking clarity about a situation you're experiencing with a particular person, asking about what is going on with that person and someone else is both rude and invasive.

Don't be intimidated by Tarot. It's not as complicated as it may seem. Dive in and start doing readings. The best way to gain confidence is to practice.

Lastly, a good question leads to a better answer. Let's explore that next.

Questions

The most unhelpful readings are often centered around one culprit: a poorly worded question. The old "Will I?" is probably the most problematic in my opinion. Why? Because it implies life is happening "to you." I firmly believe that although some things happen "to us," we are active participants in this thing called life. "Will I?" doesn't open up possibilities; instead, it says "This is what's up, and that's that" without any wiggle room. In a negatively delivered reading, this approach can lead to a self-fulfilling prophecy.

Instead of "Will I?" a better reframe is "What do I need to know about . . . ?" This question is open-ended, allows room to see where things are going, and offers advice. It is empowering for the reader and the sitter.

Another question that doesn't lend well to Tarot is "Should I . . . ?" Asking a question this way takes power out of the hands of the querent. Instead, it puts the responsibility for decision-making in the hands of the reader. A better way to ask for advice: "What can I expect if I . . . ?" Once again, this framing allows the querent to gather helpful information. This way, they can use that info to make decisions that feel right for them.

Lastly, yes/no questions aren't the best. Sometimes they can give a clear answer, but life isn't always neat or black and white. There are subtle shades of gray; and in readings about loss, grief, or caregiving, they are the least helpful of all.

Other reframes I like:

How can I . . . ?

What is the best possible outcome if I . . . ?

What am I not seeing about . . . ?

What path might help me . . . ?

There are many other ways to frame questions too. However, it's crucial for the topics in this book that you consider your ask carefully.

Practice: Try reframing these questions using the preceding tips.

When will I feel better?

Will I be able to get past this situation?

Should I move?

Am I ever going to find the right person?

Remember: focus on questions that lead to helpful information!

👁 **Pro tip:** If you're reading for someone else and they ask disempowering questions, gently guide them to the reframe. For example, say someone wants to know "Will I ever find relief from all this work?" You can simply say, "Let's look at the cards and see what you need to do to find ease." As you can see, you're not ignoring the request, but instead moving the query toward helpful guidance. In some situations, you might need to let the querent know there is a better way to frame the question. I recommend this if they insist on continuously asking "Will I?" or "Should I?" types of questions.

Now, let's explore some possible interpretations for each card. Keep in mind that they will be aligned with our topic. I'm including reversals, but it is up to you if you want to work with them or not. You can ignore them if you don't like them. Make Tarot your own.

TAROT CARD MEANINGS

I N THIS CHAPTER, we'll focus on interpretations based on the topic of this book. These interpretations were developed after many years of reading for the public. Keep in mind that these are only a guideline. The more you work with Tarot, the more likely you'll find your own meanings. So always trust your own wisdom. There are many other ways of looking at the cards. I've kept these meanings concisely associated with the focus of this book.

That being said, for some of you, these interpretations may also resonate with other concerns that are top of mind. After all, when it comes to dealing with health, caregiving, passing on, aging, and losses of all types, some of the themes of our regular life still play a role. For example, finances are often a concern when going through treatment, especially here in the United States. Therefore, it is essential to keep in mind some financial interpretations.

As I've said, when you begin working with the cards regularly, you'll develop your own meanings. Always trust your gut. If you see something that doesn't align with a so-called standard interpretation, don't hesitate to follow it and see where it leads. Your own instincts will often trump the traditional meanings in many cases.

The Major Arcana

For the Major Arcana, I've included "practices" for each card. These are simple, spiritual ways to connect with your deck. I have found these techniques are especially helpful not just to understand the deeper message behind the Majors but also to learn how to use them as a tool for spiritual support when you need it most.

To recap: the Major Arcana symbolize the bigger picture, life lessons, fate, and our spiritual journey.

The Fool

Card Number 0

Uranus

The Fool indicates a new journey. You can put the past in the past . . . and start moving toward a new life. The path has been long and hard, but now you're free. Your life is opening up to many new experiences. You'll want to take only the tools you need going forward. After all, a fresh start doesn't require much baggage. The less, the better. Consider this the first day of the rest of your life. The Fool can also represent freedom. You're leaving a situation and beginning with a clean slate. The future is yours to write. This card can also indicate the first steps on a spiritual or healing journey. You are on the precipice, a place where you must take a leap into the unknown. Let go of your preconceived notions and enter this time with a beginner's mind. Where will you go from here? What new things will you discover? These adventures are meant to be enjoyed, not feared. The possibilities are endless, but first you must trust the Universe as you step off. Trusting isn't about being naive. Instead, it's a willingness to see what may happen rather than trying to control the situation. The Fool is innocent, just as we are in any new experience. You don't need to know what's ahead, nor do you have to bring your past experiences into the situation. Let nothing color your mind as you spread your wings and welcome the new possibilities.

Reversed: Life seems stuck at the moment. Not much is changing, and you must remain patient. It's also possible you're not ready to make a change. If that is the case, give yourself as much time as you need or ask for support. If you are fearful, go within and ask yourself what is causing this. Is it the fear of loss or of not being in control? Is it because you can't see where you're going? No matter what holds you back, you can find a way to move through this energy. A risk may be required—or perhaps it's not time for risking anything. Instead, you might need to take a step back to examine how you feel and what you need to take with you before the journey begins. The Fool reversed can also mean a somber attitude that leaves no room for spontaneity or joy. Can you find playfulness at this time? Loosen up and do not fear appearing foolish.

Journaling prompt: What parts of the past can I safely release?

Practice: Take the Fool card in your hands. Breathe deeply and recall a time when you needed to have complete faith in a situation or person. Open your eyes and scan the card. What stands out? Let that become your spiritual sign from the Universe. For example, say you are drawn to the feather. So when you're out and about, look for feathers. Those are your personal messages from the Universe.

Pro tip: Sometimes, the Fool can indicate the afterlife. I've seen this card come up when a loved one wants to assure the querent they are "free" and off on a new journey. This message can be reassuring for a querent who has been struggling to accept a loss. The dog can also symbolize pets who have crossed over, which is helpful for folks who are grieving a beloved animal companion.

The Magician

Card Number 1

Mercury

Unlike the innocent Fool, the Magician has confidence. If this card shows up in your reading, it signals you have developed the will and skill to handle whatever life throws your way. Take command of the situation, and soon you'll be turning everything to your advantage. The power is with you. Of course, that doesn't mean your problem is easy. There may be tricky obstacles, which may require fancy footwork or perhaps a new way of thinking. Apply your willpower and remain focused on what you want to manifest. Then stay at it until you reach your desired goal. This is how the magic happens. The Magician is a link between heaven and earth—as above, so below. That could mean a miracle is on the way, or you're trying everything possible to change a situation. Notice all the tools on the table; this symbolizes having everything you need to reach the goal. You simply need to believe in your own power. If you're not sure how to use those tools, experiment. Test out various things until you see results. Be creative and open to new ways of doing things. This approach could lead to a bold discovery. Sometimes this card can indicate being an advocate for yourself. Are you making your wishes known? How can you stand in your power at this time? Lastly, the Magician can symbolize a skilled person who may be helpful at this time.

Reversed: This could be a disempowering period. It may be hard to focus, or perhaps you're overwhelmed. It's also possible you don't have the tools you need. Instead of trying to carry the whole burden, ask for help. You do not have to try to do it all. Sometimes the Magician reversed can symbolize the magic is within yourself. Rather than looking for an outside source, you might want to invest your energy into inner work. This approach may help you make peace with your current situation. Mary K. Greer says this reversal can mean a "magician or medicine person." However, it can also warn of an untrained person or quack. Be sure to get a second opinion if anything seems off.

Journaling prompt: How can I empower myself in this situation?

Practice: Have you ever experienced a situation where a health-care practitioner or other authority figure talked down to you? If so, you need the Magician's energy. Here's what to do: the next time you are scheduled for a visit, spend time meditating on the Magician card. Visualize the red robe, the infinity symbol, and the powerful stance. Then, picture yourself in the Magician's setting, wearing the colorful cloak and wielding the wand. What does that feel like? Breathe in that power, and when you're ready, open your eyes. Keep that energy with you and be an advocate for yourself. Remain confident as you stand in your power. You are the ultimate authority of you.

I turned into this vibe after a recent situation with a health-care provider. The new assistant was rough, and I bore through a horrible experience with tears streaming down my face. I was in pain but said nothing. The next day, I spent a little time with the Magician. Once I felt connected to the energy, I emailed the office to complain and tell them exactly how I wanted to be cared for going forward. This is Magician energy in action.

Pro tip: While it's important to encourage people to speak up for themselves, you don't want to suggest ignoring doctors' orders. Never play that role!

HIGH PRIESTESS.

High Priestess

Card Number 2

Moon

Intuition guides you at this time. If you feel funny about a situation or person, go with it. Trust your inner wisdom; it may be the key to your healing. It may also be the time to apply spiritual practices to your situation. Step away from the daily grind to care for your spirit. Rest, meditate, or spend time journaling. Doing so can help bring you back into balance. I've also seen this card symbolize time spent in seclusion (such as visiting an ashram) or quarantine. Sometimes the High Priestess can represent a spiritual healer or medical intuitive who plays a vital role in your situation. This card is also associated with messages from the other side. The curtain symbolizes the veil between worlds, while the Moon represents our subconscious and conscious self. Psychic experiences are possible but must be melded with practical experience. In some cases, this card can warn about a hidden problem or agenda. Something will be revealed at a later date.

Reversed: You're coming out of a period of isolation and getting back into the swing of things. It feels good to be part of the world again! Sometimes the High Priestess can also mean difficulty trusting your intuition. You have a feeling about something, but you ignore it. Later on, you wish you had paid attention. This reversal can also indicate a secret revealed. I've also seen it symbolize a fatalistic attitude, where you feel you have no control over your circumstances. In that case, know there are always choices available. Don't give up.

Journaling prompt: What is Spirit trying to tell me right now?

Practice: Find all the cards with Moons in your deck. Moons symbolize change, the unconscious, fear, illusions, and cycles. What does the Moon reveal in each of those cards? Can you find similar meanings in every card that features a Moon?

The Empress

Card Number 3

Venus

The Empress is often associated with the mother figure in your life. This person is someone who provides nurturing, such as a parent, partner, or health-care practitioner. However, it's also possible you're playing that role somehow. For example, you may be the caregiver for a child or elder. The Empress always provides loving support, whether you're receiving help or tending to other people's needs.

Sometimes, this card is more aligned with pleasure, indulgence, creativity, or good health. The energy is comfortable, relaxed, and pampered. Perhaps this is a time when you are practicing deep self-care. If so, this practice could positively contribute to your well-being. The Empress can also mean patience. Seeds have been planted, and they are beginning to sprout. Soon, there will be a big harvest at your feet. You cannot force this to happen. Like a child being born, the energy must be right before pushing. Trust that everything is moving along in divine time; it won't be long before you're holding new life in your hands. Of course, the Empress is the fertility or pregnancy card, so it can mean that—or anything you're trying to birth. In some cases, this card can also indicate being so preoccupied with your situation that you begin to lose sight of the beauty around you. Don't forget to stop and smell the roses.

Reversed: I often see the Empress reversed as mother issues. For example, if you're taking care of your mom, she may be uncooperative or manipulative. Or perhaps she's in control of matters, and you don't like how she runs the show. Either way, the situation can only be resolved if all sides stop taking things personally. Until that happens, the drama may be ongoing. This reversal can also mean neglect—as in neglecting your body or not caring for the folks depending on you. For some, it's the archetype for the caregiver who doesn't make any time for self-care. If that's you, you need to dial back your duties if you want to avoid burnout or resentment. I've also seen this card symbolize a time when you lack joy and cannot find pleasure. In this case, you feel emotionally spent. Or maybe you're needy to the point of codependence. Either way, the balance is lost.

Finally, this card might indicate reproductive issues or a need for more care in a health reading.

Journaling prompt: How do I meet my needs while caring for others?

 **Practice:** Embody the energy of the Empress by creating a self-care day for yourself. Clear your calendar, soak in the tub, get a massage, and eat foods you love. You can also practice her loving energy by sending a care package to someone struggling.

👁 **Pro tip:** Sometimes Tarot readers play the role of the Empress with their clients. But you must be careful you don't cross a line by creating codependence. While a caring nature is essential for Tarot readers, getting too involved in your clients' lives will blur boundaries and impact your objectivity. So keep your readings clean by maintaining healthy boundaries at all times.

The Emperor

Card Number 4

Aries

The Emperor sits firmly on his stone throne, an ankh in one hand and a golden globe in the other. His long beard suggests maturity, and the hint of armor peeking out from the red robe shows protection. This card is associated with security, wisdom, and control. When this card appears in a reading, it can symbolize the father or another authority figure in your life, such as a specialist. They are stern, but you can trust them to take control of matters. Of course, you can be in this role: you may be handling someone's business or taking care of your family. This is the "provider" who makes sure the realm is safe. Whether sitting on the throne or relying on someone else, this card says, "I've got this handled." The Emperor may be interested in new conquests eventually, but for now, stability is what matters. As long as the situation is secured, this person is content to sit tight. What structures do you have in place at this time? Do you have routines to keep you feeling safe? Are you taking care of your affairs or hoping someone else will step up? You have to decide whether you're in charge or dependent on another person. Of course, even if you are under someone else's care, you are still the authority of your life. You do have agency. This card can also show up when you need to set limits. Perhaps you must assert your boundaries, or maybe you need to explore other options. It's okay to be the boss of your world.

Reversed: A situation reaches a critical point. Things seem to be spiraling downward fast. You feel vulnerable. More help is needed. For some, this represents a loss of control. You're no longer in charge and must surrender to whatever is happening. The Emperor reversed can also warn of being overconfident. You think you've got this in the bag, but it's far from a sure thing. It's best to remain humble. This reversal can also point to a tendency to resist change unless you're the one in the driver's seat. Do you really need to be in control? Does the current situation warrant a new Emperor? It's also an excellent time to reflect on your relationship with power. Is it healthy? Do you abuse your position, or do you allow others to push you around? Find the balance between being in command and respecting other people's differences. In some cases, this reversal can mean anger or oppression. If you take that route, you might alienate the people who want to help you.

Journaling prompt: What would life look like if I let go of control just this once?

Practice: Securing the fortress is the Emperor's domain. Channel this energy by creating security right now. That might mean seeing an expert or perhaps getting your papers in order. New structures will give you peace of mind. (Psst, no shame in wanting to have everything under control!) It's good to be king!

Pro tip: Take control of your readings by always letting your querent know up front what to expect in their session with you. For example, you might want to let them know about your method or ethics. Taking this approach will set expectations and lead to fewer boundary issues.

The Hierophant

Card Number 5

Taurus

The Hierophant can represent a teacher, mentor, therapist, spiritual counselor, guru, or expert. It's the wise person you turn to when you need advice. Who plays that role in your life? And what wisdom do you need at this time? Lay your questions and concerns at their feet. This will help you find solace no matter what is happening in your world. Of course, you may be in the Hierophant's seat. Others may be relying on your wise counsel. In that case, be sure to stick to your ethics. Set the right example, and you'll inspire others. Spiritual practices may play a vital role in your healing now. Prayer, meditation, time spent in holy places, or any other practice will provide peace. The Hierophant can also symbolize a rite of passage or a ritual. In some cases, it may suggest reviewing your traditions for guidance. Sometimes this card can indicate receiving a blessing. That could come in the form of an "all clear" from a doctor. Of course, because the Hierophant is associated with obedience, it could simply be saying, "Follow the doctor's orders."

Reversed: It might be wise to explore unorthodox approaches to your situation. A death doula, naturopath, or holistic doctor may have suggestions to support your current care. If you break with tradition, make sure you are taking precautions. This reversal could indicate blind faith—that feeling everything will work out, no matter what. It can also warn of a spiritual teacher or counselor giving dubious advice. If something feels off, it may be in your best interest to get a second opinion. The Hierophant reversed can also mean intolerance toward other people's beliefs. For example, the religious hypocrite who preaches love but is hostile to anyone who doesn't fit their definition of what is "good."

Journaling prompt: What spiritual traditions might support me at this time?

Practice: Has it been too long since you've visited a trusted spiritual advisor? Make an appointment with your favorite Hierophant: a pastor, rabbi, therapist, counselor, or Tarot reader. This support can help you move through your situation with grace.

The Lovers

Card Number 6

Gemini

A choice needs to be made. There may be a risk or temptation involved. You must take your time and listen to what your guides are telling you. Gather the information and let your heart decide: it knows what it wants. The Lovers can also indicate working with a helper or partner to heal or deal with a situation. You have the support you need at this time. Love is present, and it has the power to transform. In a health question, this could mean getting a second opinion or working with different modalities. What other options are available? Have you explored every possible avenue? For relationships, this card can indicate love in all forms: romantic, platonic, or familial. Maybe you're enjoying their company, or perhaps healing is taking place. An olive branch has been offered, opening the door for forgiveness. Vulnerability is necessary, which means being completely open and putting judgement on hold. The Lovers can also symbolize a message from the divine . . . or a departed loved one. This is one of my "guardian angel" cards.

Reversed: A lack of support. Your loved ones are not there when you need them the most. Or perhaps you have pushed them away. Are you unwilling to let people in? Is your heart closed off? If so, how can you change this? This may be an excellent time to seek reconciliation if you have cut people off. The Lovers reversed can also indicate indecision. Suddenly, you're unsure which way to go or which option is best. Maybe an old decision is coming back to haunt you, or you're dismissing the importance of a choice you're about to make. Take a deep breath and consider all sides and possible consequences. A mindful approach will heal the past and prevent future regrets. In some cases, the Lovers reversed can mean you're struggling with trust issues, especially with authority figures. Something has happened, and now you're losing faith.

Journaling prompt: What choices can I make right now to move my situation into a better place?

 **Practice:** The next time you need to make an important decision, explore your options, and see what your heart has to say. What feels like love? That's your answer. This is a great way to tap into the energy of the Lovers.

Pro tip: Sometimes people want another person present when they are getting a reading. In some cases, this makes sense. For example, you would want to have a guardian in the room if you're reading for a minor. Other times, having another person there can be distracting. You'll have to use your common sense and intuition to determine whether it feels right . . . or not.

The Chariot

Card Number 7

Cancer

The Chariot is a card of discipline and willpower. No matter how challenging the road may be, you can overcome anything if you put your mind to it. The power is in your hands, and you are sitting in the perfect vehicle to reach your goal safely. In other words, everything is under control, and progress is assured. The Chariot says: you're in charge of your body, environment, and habits. You've got this! This card can also symbolize a new journey, perhaps one that is spiritual in nature. Or maybe it's physical travel—perhaps you're visiting a loved one who lives at a distance or taking a much-needed trip away. In some cases, this means playing the role of a warrior. You must don your battle gear and fight the good fight. A win is possible if you give it your all. In a spiritual reading, the Chariot shows progress on your life's journey. A responsible attitude is moving you toward your goal. Lastly, it may mean you must take time to understand the past before moving on. Do not charge ahead until you know the history and the lessons.

Reversed: A loss of control. The situation is no longer in your hands. You must let go and put your faith in other people. Letting go could be hard, but if you want to make progress, it might be better for someone else to take over. The Chariot reversed can also mean a setback or a reckless attitude. A desire for change may cause you to ignore common sense. You're running wild or acting irresponsibly. Or maybe you're trying to force issues or assert yourself where you're not wanted. If this is the case, you might create new problems. This reversal can also indicate an inward or spiritual journey instead of a physical one. In some situations, this card can mean an accident or misstep.

Journaling prompt: What progress can I acknowledge right now?

Practice: Recall a time when you had to apply willpower to change a situation. What was that like? Did you find it hard or not? Journal about your feelings on discipline.

Pro tip: The only way to get good at Tarot is constant practice. Not just reading your own daily card, but also reading for as many folks as you can. The more people you read for, the more likely you'll encounter various situations that will stretch your intuitive muscles and Tarot interpretations!

Strength

Card Number 8

Leo

The Strength card is always a sound card to see in readings about health: it symbolizes overcoming a hard battle. Your strength prevails . . . or you find it at last! You have the power and the will to survive. You've got everything under control . . . or will soon enough. Sometimes the Strength card refers to a support system. The right help is around you at this time. Remember, the help could come from people in your life or spirit guides. For example, this could be a guardian angel, a sign of divine protection. Or that angel could come in the form of a loved one who is always by your side. It's possible you could be playing that role too. In that case, you're the gracious caregiver, always willing to be of service, no matter how difficult the situation may be. This card can also indicate a test of courage. You're about to learn how powerful you are. Remain resolute, trusting in your ability to handle whatever tests you're given. Your determination will pay off soon enough. Tackle the hard stuff but don't lose your soft side. Finally, Strength can also represent the battle between living passionately while taming the beast within. There is nothing wrong with having strong feelings, provided you keep them in check.

Reversed: You've lost the will to fight. You're giving up—or letting fear dictate the situation. This is when you are losing hope and need more support. You may be overwhelmed or trying to do too many things at once. It's also possible someone else is making things difficult. In that case, Strength reversed says: you need to set a boundary. Sometimes this reversal means lacking the courage or integrity to do the right thing. Instead, you sit back and hope someone else handles the situation. This passivity will only cause problems. It's better to be brave and take responsibility. In some cases, this could also mean the lesser desires are taking over, and you've lost control. For example, situations such as addiction or other self-destructive habits. Because of the connection to Leo, the reversal can also mean trouble with the spine or heart chakra.

Journaling prompt: When have I felt strong?

Practice: Take the Strength card out of the deck and put it somewhere you can see it daily when you're going through the hard stuff. Create an affirmation such as "I am powerful" and state that whenever you look at the card. Say this affirmation out loud in a positive, courageous voice.

The Strength card is your reminder that you are stronger than you know.

The Hermit

Card Number 9

Virgo

The Hermit sheds light on what is possible. They've gone through the darkness and have spiritual knowledge to share. When this card arrives, it's a sign that you have found wisdom through a trial. You're the expert and can now be a lantern in the dark for other people. In some readings, the Hermit symbolizes a teacher, mentor, counselor, or healer. This person may provide the proper guidance when you need it most. If you are struggling, take your problems to them. Of course, it's possible you could be playing this role for someone else. Trust that you have the wisdom they need. In some readings this card says: solitude is necessary at this time. You must pull away from the world to focus on your inner life. You can do this by spending time alone or retreating to a sacred place. What's important is that you allow yourself to rest. Peace and quiet will restore your sense of wellness. Of course, the shadow side of this practice is a feeling of isolation. If you've cut off the world, you might experience loneliness. Lastly, this is also an excellent time to reflect on your current circumstances. How can you take a spiritual approach to the current issue? What does your inner wisdom have to say about matters?

Reversed: You're emerging from the cocoon after a period of isolation or recovery. Now you're back in the world, feeling healed and ready to start a new cycle. Of course, this reversal can also symbolize trouble with wise elders or teachers. Maybe they are giving you poor advice . . . or none at all. Sometimes this card means you want to be alone but can't be due to responsibilities. I've also seen this card mean feeling old and out of sorts. When the Hermit shows up reversed, you may not feel that you know what's up . . . but you do. The other interpretation I have found to be accurate is "not learning from your past mistakes." If you keep doing something that doesn't work, why do you expect a different outcome?

Journaling prompt: How does solitude help me?

Practice: Take a weekend away for solo pursuits. Spend time in an ashram or spa. Meditate in a forest. Go to the library and read books in silence. This is a great way to restore your balance and tune into the Hermit's solitude.

Pro tip: Sometimes you may find you feel complacent or "blah" with your Tarot deck. In that case, it's wise to take a break! You might want to leave the cards alone for a while or try a new deck. Either choice will help you come back to the cards with a fresh perspective.

Wheel of Fortune

Card Number 10

Jupiter

Everything is about to change when the Wheel shows up—usually for the better. For example, an opportunity may arise, or you might be on the road to manifesting a cherished goal. But there is also a bit of unpredictability at this time. You must have faith. Do not let the changes scare you; instead, lean into them. There is opportunity there. Fate is spinning a new tale, and a period of adjustment is ahead. Whatever is happening is due to decisions made in the past. However, momentum is gathering, and soon you'll see where things are going. The Wheel of Fortune can also mean the laws of karma are at work. Something is set in motion, paving the way for a new future. Roll with it. Your situation is evolving into something completely different. Of course, if you do not like the direction unfolding, this is your time to pivot. You can always make new decisions . . . and the ones you make now could be critical. Choose wisely. Sometimes this card refers to the universal cycles, which are always in motion. As my wise friend Reverend Joe once said, "The only thing that is unchanging is change." Nothing ever remains the same, even though it may sometimes feel that way. The Wheel of Fortune can also be a reminder to stay calm and go with the flow of life. It's better to trust the Universe rather than allow doubt to take the Wheel.

Reversed: Your situation stalls. You're in limbo and need to wait it out. Or perhaps things are in a stop-start mode. These circumstances can be aggravating and anxiety-inducing. Try to roll with it as best as you can. Even this stagnancy isn't forever. The Wheel is constantly in motion, and at some point, life will start to move forth again. This reversal can also indicate poor decision-making. Are you repeating the past? What can you learn from those old mistakes now that you didn't learn then? Is there a way to avoid cycling through these lessons? Sometimes this card shows a situation from the past arising once again. Or perhaps you feel rudderless without a sense of where things are going. In some readings, this reversal could mean fighting change by digging in your heels, even though the current situation isn't beneficial. You'll also want to watch out for victim mentality or engaging in a pity party at this time. Lastly, if you're not doing what you need to do to get well, why would you expect a change in your circumstance?

Journaling prompt: What changes can I accept . . . or make?

Practice: I adore talismans and good luck charms. Wearing them makes me feel lucky, especially during trying times. Find a piece of jewelry that embodies the feeling of opportunity. If you can locate one that looks like a Wheel, even better. Keep it close to your heart and have faith the Universe has your back. (It does.)

Justice

Card Number 11

Libra

Justice indicates a big decision is on the table. You must weigh all options with care before taking action. For example, you might be choosing between two or more promising opportunities. Or perhaps your situation is delicate, and your decisions could impact your future for a long time. Nothing can happen until you've done your research. Take your time, explore the possibilities, and when you feel confident, make your choice. A mindful approach will stack the odds in your favor. Sometimes this card symbolizes contracts or legal issues. Suppose you're negotiating a deal or signing essential papers. In that case, you'll want to read all the details to understand the consequences. Justice can also symbolize results from past decisions. Karma. In questions about health, this card says: seek balance. If you're not sure about a current diagnosis, you may want to seek a second opinion. Lastly, Justice means taking responsibility for your life. If you do the right thing now, tomorrow will be better.

Reversed: A lack of options—or choices are being made for you. A situation becomes unbalanced, leaving you feeling uncertain. Legal issues and red tape could be putting you in a difficult position. Suddenly, you're hanging in the balance, waiting for an authority figure to decide. Life feels unfair. You don't have enough support, which throws your life out of whack. Justice reversed can also mean injustice or a lack of integrity. Is your moral compass having trouble pointing in the right direction? If so, how can you rectify this situation? You might have to take the high road, even if it is hard for a while.

Journaling prompt: What decision would move me in a better direction right now?

Practice: Do you have your legal affairs in order? If something happened to you, would your loved ones know your wishes? Be like the Justice card and organize all your essential papers. You'll feel good, and your family will too.

Pro tip: Never promise something you cannot deliver as a Tarot reader. For example, claiming to be 100 percent accurate is false. Always be up front about your abilities, skill level, and the fact you're only human with the potential to make mistakes sometimes.

The Hanged One

Card Number 12

Neptune

Nothing much is happening right now. You are forced to wait. Is that such a bad thing? Not really. Sure, it's uncomfortable, but sometimes we have no choice. Soon you'll emerge with a different perspective . . . and a new truth. In fact, you might see the light at last. The Hanged One can also indicate a sacrifice. You might be called to give something up for a higher purpose. This could be a short-term sacrifice that leads to long-term happiness. Sometimes this card is associated with a test of faith. If that is the case, try your best to see the spiritual message in your situation. If you're reacting negatively, reframe the situation. See if you can find the good. In some cases, this card means taking an unorthodox approach to a problem. Instead of doing the usual, a fresh approach may be better. The Hanged One is also associated with escapism or playing the role of a martyr. Your hands are tied, and you cannot seem to find the escape hatch. Perhaps it is better to let go and let Spirit take over. Or ask for help.

Reversed: Things begin to move. No more waiting—this is time for action. You're landing on your feet after a period of suspension. Your faith pays off, and you can begin anew. The Hanged One reversed can also warn of a useless sacrifice. You gave up everything, but for what? Maybe no one realizes how much you put on the line. Nothing worked out the way you wanted, or you're not getting the credit you deserve. You're ready to give up and let go of your vision. This reversal can also mean a spiritual turning point, depending on the rest of the reading.

Journaling prompt: What can I release once and for all?

Practice: Waiting rooms in doctors' or dentists' offices are often stressful. The next time you find yourself in one, think of the Hanged One and channel their relaxed, calm attitude. Visualize a golden halo of light around your head. Breathe deeply. Notice how much better you feel when you approach any stressful situation like this.

Pro tip: Timing is the hardest thing to predict in a Tarot reading, yet it's often the thing folks want the most. They are also hoping you'll say something will happen quickly because no one wants to wait! Be careful about giving exact dates, especially around tender topics. I have found this tends to create more anxiety than relief.

Death

Card Number 13

Scorpio

Let's start by saying: the Death card does not mean literal death. Please keep this point in mind, especially when you read for others. Instead, the Death card means something is coming to an end, paving the way for a new life. Change is often difficult for folks to accept, and sometimes it's scary. But now is the time to acknowledge something is on the way out. Let go and make space for new things to materialize. This card means transformation and metamorphosis. You're becoming a different person, or a situation in your life is being altered profoundly. What cycle in your life is about to change? What are you willing to release? Shed the old thoughts, habits, attitudes, patterns, or possessions that no longer serve you. Clear the past and step fully into your future. In some cases, this card could mean unfinished mourning. Some underlying sadness needs to be addressed. If you're wearing a mask, take it off. Let the real you emerge.

Reversed: Everything is up in the air. Nothing seems to be changing, so you're forced to wait or accept things as they are. Perhaps you're resisting change . . . and pushing back on the inevitable. In that case, you must ask yourself where fear may be playing a role. Is it a comfort zone? Or do you worry you're not in control of the changes ahead? Is this making you hold on to something or someone you've outgrown? If so, what can you do to turn this behavior around? Death reversed can also mean coming out of a period of darkness. At last, you're ready to start anew. Instead of hanging in the past, you're creating a bright future. This card can also mean recovery or a near-death experience that leads to a new perspective.

Journaling prompt: What changes might help me at this time?

 **Practice:** Have you ever contemplated your mortality? If so, what are your beliefs? Does thinking about this topic give you a feeling of dread or peace? Or are you simply curious? Ponder these questions and then journal your thoughts.

👁 **Pro tip:** If someone asks you to predict their date of death, do not entertain this notion. It crosses an ethical line and can create unnecessary worry.

Temperance

Card Number 14

Sagittarius

A beautiful angel stands on a rock, one toe in the water, as they pour water from one chalice to another. In the background, a path emerges with a golden crown on the horizon. Every time I draw this card, I feel immediately at peace. It's one of the best cards to see because it means situations are healing. Something new is rising out of the ashes, and soon you'll find a way to make the best out of what's left. Temperance is the ability to find calm in the midst of chaos. Rather than giving in to fear, this card says: you can be grace under pressure. You might be trying more than one modality or mixing different paths to see what might work best. This experimentation might yield surprising results. Sometimes this card can mean getting your affairs in order. It may be time to plan for the future or prepare for a journey. Be clear on your wishes to the people who love you the most. Doing so will give you a clear conscience and the ability to move on without worry. In a spiritual reading, Temperance could mean reflecting on past mistakes and finding the lessons. It's also one of the "guardian angel" cards in the deck. In a mediumship reading, it can symbolize a time when the dearly departed "get their wings."

Reversed: Suddenly, everything is thrown off-balance. The flow is disrupted, and any chance for healing stalls. Nothing seems to be moving, which leads to frustration. It's possible you may be dealing with a situation that comes and goes, or stress-induced disorders.

How can you find calm at this time? It may be essential for your well-being. Temperance reversed can also mean overindulging or overdoing. Addictive tendencies could spiral out of control. You'll need to address these behaviors if you're self-medicating by abusing substances, gambling, compulsively shopping, or self-harming. Consulting with a trusted advisor can get you back on the right path. It's never too late to turn things around. Sometimes this reversal can mean a spiritual crisis. If you feel lost, your angels have never left your side. Call on them now; they will assist you.

Journaling prompt: What can bring balance into my situation?

Practice: It's believed that angels send signs, often in numbers, such as 11. Start paying attention to random numbers that seem to pop up from time to time. Who might be trying to send a message to you?

The Devil

Card Number 15

Capricorn

The Devil is one of those cards no one seems to like. The traditional meanings don't make it appealing either: addiction, being stuck, or bondage. If this card shows up, you might just be in a dark place at the moment. But the chains that bind you are loose, and there is a way out. The Devil may look scary, but he's not in control. You are. Examine your situation and how you've arrived at this place. This holds the key to your liberation. Sometimes this card can mean shadow work—facing the dark night of the soul. On the other side of this is spiritual growth. Because sometimes you need to go through hell before finding your way back. In some cases, this card could mean losing your way or getting lost in despair, anger, or obsessive thinking. Again: there is an exit. You can change your situation by admitting the problem and seeking support. At times, this card means arguments over money or material goods. It can also mean toxic relationships that are difficult to extricate yourself from. On the other hand, this card can mean devilish humor or mischief. Lastly, it can mean choosing between the Devil you know and the one you don't. The path to victory isn't clear or easy. Choose well.

Reversed: You're free at last! Whatever seemed to be holding you back is gone. Or maybe you liberated yourself. Either way, the light at the end of the tunnel has arrived. Help is available, and decisions are crystal clear. Now you know exactly what you need to do to remedy the situation. Sometimes this reversal means letting go of a problem or problematic person. It's also possible you found the courage to face your own demons, and now you can release them once and for all. Finally, you can find your spiritual path after a long, challenging period. This is one of the best cards to see if you are recovering or attempting to get clean. In some cases, the Devil reversed may mean giving up the struggle. Surrender and let fate sort it out.

Journaling prompt: What is holding me back?

Practice: The Devil is a scary card to see, but if you look closely, you'll see the figure holds a flame, which provides light in the dark. Think of a time when all felt lost, but you found your way. Journal about that experience.

Pro tip: Some folks come from backgrounds where Tarot was seen as the "work of the devil," so it's no surprise they might get scared when this card shows up. If you sense someone might have that mindset, please use a neutral deck instead. This will take the fear out of the reading and lead to a better experience for the querent (and you!).

The Tower

Card Number 16

Mars

Suddenly, everything comes crashing down. The stability is lost, and you must let it all go. But were things as secure as you thought? Probably not. The structures were faulty or built on a weak foundation. Now you must surrender to this change, even though the future seems uncertain. While it may appear your world is crashing, there is also enlightenment. The Tower is the wake-up call, the moment you see the light, leading to accelerated spiritual growth. It's also possible you may need to leave a situation in a hurry. In that case, don't hesitate. Get out of there as swiftly as possible. This card can also mean a downfall or moment when you are brought to your knees. The ego receives a significant shake-up, and what you think about yourself will change. You must humble yourself, let go of pride, and be willing to take responsibility. In some readings, the Tower can indicate "losing your top." If your emotions are blowing up, the air will get cleared. Or maybe you're clearing away energetic debris or decluttering your surroundings. For example, people at the end of life often give away their possessions. On occasion, this card has shown up to indicate an accident.

Reversed: There may still be drama, but it's less stressful. Perhaps the first shockwave already occurred, and this is an aftershock. You can rebuild now because the dust is settled. Or you already went down this path before, so you know what to expect. Either way, the Tower reversed says: you know what you're doing. In some cases, this reversal means freedom. You're no longer bound by anything or anyone. You can move about at will. Sometimes it can indicate recovery from an accident or illness. The worst is passing, and you're in remission.

Journaling prompt: How can I improve this situation?

Practice: When we receive news that shocks us to the core, it's always a "Tower moment." Consider a time when you went through something like this. What did you learn from that situation? Were you able to trust the Universe at that time, or was your faith shattered? Journal about your Tower moment.

The Star

Card Number 17

Aquarius

The Star indicates healing has begun. After tremendous challenges, you are in a period of regeneration. A new you is emerging, and hope is returning. As you make peace with the past, you can feel faith in the future. What's done is done; now you understand what happened in a new light. This is the calm after a storm or stabilization after upheaval. Renewal, purification, or baptism. Sometimes this card can mean revealing your true self. You don't have to hide any part of yourself. Instead, you can be open, honest, and free. If you have neglected your spirituality, this card says: start it up again. It's never too late to reconnect with your spiritual life. The Star is also a card of recognition. At last, you're in the spotlight, ready to receive your just rewards. You could also be in the spotlight as a role model for what is possible. Another way of looking at this card is wish fulfillment. Something you wanted is coming to fruition. A miracle. Lastly, the Star is another one of the guardian angel cards. Someone is looking out for you.

Reversed: This reversal can mean losing faith in a situation. You're depleted and tired. You've been giving too much of yourself. The problems seem to be ongoing with no end in sight. How can you remain hopeful when the situation doesn't improve? If life is stagnant, where can you find a reason to keep going? But watch that you're not giving up too soon. Something is happening under the surface, and with time, you'll see a chance to start anew. The Star reversed can mean depression or relapse. If you're experiencing either, you'll want to seek help. In some cases, this could mean you're fearful of being dependent on others for your basic needs, or you can no longer take care of yourself. Maybe you've lost the will to live. Again, this may be your green light to ask for and accept help. For caregivers, this reversal means you've been doing too much for others.

Journaling prompt: What needs healing right now?

Practice: The Star is one of the classic wish cards in the deck. If you could make any wish right now, what would that be? Write it down on a piece of paper and draw your own rendition of the Star. Then, put it in a purse, wallet, or something you always carry with you. Trust that your guides are working overtime to help you manifest your wish.

👁 **Pro tip:** Never let a client walk away from the Tarot table feeling hopeless. Even in difficult situations, you can use the cards to find solutions or solace. Treat your Tarot deck like a tool for healing, and it will become that.

The Moon

Card Number 18

Pisces

When the Moon shows up, nothing is clear. Everything seems to be in flux. This means it's hard to see the outcome or what choice you should make. You'll need to take your time and gather more information. Or you'll have to rely on your instincts. Pay attention to how you feel and let it guide you into making excellent choices. Of course, emotions could be pulling you in many different directions. You're being driven, but to what? Proceed with courage and curiosity. All will be revealed in due time. This journey is without a clear path. It could also be a doorway to the unknown. You may feel you're being guided by something greater than yourself. All you can do is go forth and trust that you'll find your way. Imagination is active at this time, and while this could inspire your creativity, it can also lead to irrational fears. You'll need to keep your anxiety in check, or it will immobilize you. For health readings, the Moon says the situation has an underlying issue that needs to be examined. This issue could be physical, emotional, or spiritual. Or you are being kept in the dark. For example, a health-care practitioner won't communicate what's going on. Take nothing at face value. Dig for facts.

Reversed: Clarity arrives. You can see what's up. A path is laid out for you, and the options are spelled out. Instead of letting your instincts guide you, now you have the facts. The facts might give you comfort because at least you know exactly what to expect. There are no shortcuts, no hidden agendas, or problems. It's all out in the open, which means you can make solid, confident decisions. Sometimes this reversal can mean old memories being retrieved from someplace deep inside your consciousness. Or dreams that reveal important messages. This could be a dream of a loved one who passed over to the other side. A statement from the dead, astral travel, or past-life memories. The Star reversed can also mean addiction, hidden habits, or recovery from trauma, depending on the question and other cards. It can also indicate mood swings or ignoring the shadow.

Journaling prompt: What am I not seeing in this situation?

 **Practice:** Go outside late at night when the Moon is full. Get very quiet and listen. Listen for sounds around you and pay attention to what your inner voice is saying. Can you find communion with both the outer world and your inner world? This is the Moon in action.

The Sun

Card Number 19

Sun

The Sun is one of the most positive cards to see in the deck. When it turns up, it means good things are happening. You have a chance to start over, or you may be achieving a cherished goal. Either way, life is good, and you have many reasons to celebrate. It's your moment to shine! The Sun signifies joy, happiness, enlightenment, and abundance. It also means vitality and good health. You're on the mend! If you've been unwell, your health improves, or you're in remission. A cure has been found. This is an excellent card to see in a question about children. The Sun brings clarity: a light is shone on the truth—you can see what is up, and nothing is hidden. You have absolute clarity, giving you the power to make good choices.

Reversed: The Sun reversed is still a positive card but somewhat muted. Instead of a big celebration, you might be rejoicing over a small step forward. Or maybe you're cautiously optimistic about a situation. It's also possible someone is giving you false hope. The healing has begun, but it's slow going. The Sun reversed can also mean something isn't working as well as you hoped, which may prod you into seeking other options. This card can indicate burnout too. You're exhausted and need to rest. Or you're surviving instead of thriving. In some cases, this card can mean depression. You're feeling unhappy with the way things are going and cannot find joy in your situation. A reversed Sun can indicate retirement. It may be time to step away from the spotlight and let someone else have the main stage. Pass on the torch to the younger generation. Lastly, this card might indicate you need to heal the inner child.

Journaling prompt: What might make me feel joyful right now?

Practice: The Sun represents the child in all of us. Do something that reminds you of a time when you were young and joyful. Visit a playground and hang on the monkey bars. Look at a favorite picture book. Eat an ice cream cone . . . and make it a double scoop. It feels good to play again!

Pro tip: When reading for young folks, don't assume they don't have concerns about heavy topics such as grief. They do, and they need a safe space to talk about it. Tarot is perfect for opening up a gentle dialogue about how they feel. Be sure to treat their concerns and feelings as seriously as you would an adult's.

Judgement

Card Number 20

Pluto

Judgement is the card of rebirth: the old life is being shed to make way for a new beginning. You are getting a new life. Let go of the old so you can rise up. Like a hot air balloon, you must release the heavy weight to ascend. Judgement can also mean coming to terms with your situation. Maybe you're ready to forgive or atone for your past transgressions. Or perhaps you're accepting your fate. What's done is done. You can accept the consequences, no matter what they may be. This card is also associated with transforming a situation after a crisis. Something happened, and life will never be the same. This is a card of reincarnation: you may be retrieving past-life memories or contemplating what you want your next life to be like. Regeneration of the soul. Healing the old wounds or wounds from past lives. The Judgement card can mean your prayers are answered, or you're enlightened. It's the dawning of a new perspective as you peel away the old, dead ways of thinking. A rite of passage. Sometimes Judgement is a wake-up call or a time when you must make a significant decision. You can see the light . . . and find the best way. This is another one of the guardian angel cards, and it sometimes brings a message from the other side.

Reversed: You're unwilling to change. So you stay in a situation long past its due date. You cannot ask for help. Maybe you refuse to accept responsibility for past mistakes. You blame everyone else instead. Or you're making all the wrong decisions and listening to bad advice. This reversal can indicate an unwillingness to try a new approach when it might make a real difference. Of course, Judgement reversed is refusing to heed the call or choosing to ignore red flags. Some readings could indicate unexpected healing just when things looked dire. I've also seen this card represent making decisions under duress or being overly critical.

Journaling prompt: What can I accept at this time?

Practice: If you look back over your life, you may recognize times when you've hurt other people. The Judgement card is often associated with forgiveness. Reach back to someone in the past and apologize. Take responsibility for your role without expecting forgiveness. Create your own clean slate by acknowledging your past mistakes.

Pro tip: Be careful when it comes to suggesting forgiveness work to your clients. Some may not be ready to hear that, while others may have situations that feel unforgivable. Your job is not to judge, but to provide a safe space to process those feelings.

The World

Card Number 21

Saturn

The World says: you've learned your earthly lesson and have completed your spiritual graduation. This is the grand finale. You've made it! Now you can close this chapter and prepare for a new one. In a health reading, this means feeling good. Take care of your body and listen deeply to what it needs. You're enjoying your life. You feel whole, and all is right in your world. There is help available, and you are getting what you need. Your angels are in your corner. This card can also indicate a time when you tie up loose ends. Integration or achieving unity. Sometimes it can mean traveling the world or checking things off the bucket list. Lastly, it signals rebirth.

Reversed: The journey is delayed. Progress is stalled, and there is not much you can do but wait. You might feel unprotected or like people shield you from the truth. What can you do to ensure you're meeting your needs if you don't feel supported? It's also possible you're holding on, afraid to let go. This is keeping you stagnant. Let go and let Spirit lead the way. Your karmic debts are paid, so there is no need to hold on to the past. Sometimes the World reversed symbolizes a womb or a time when you want to return to the Source. You want safety, so it's easier to head back to a familiar place. Sometimes, this reversal can indicate a time when you think the world revolves around you. You might miss the bigger picture if you're caught up in your own world. Other interpretations could be traveling for health-care or spiritual renewal, a community illness, or airborne disease. Lastly, it can also suggest partial healing. It's not perfect, but at least you're seeing some improvement.

Journaling prompt: What can I do to ensure my world feels safe?

Practice: If you had to rewrite your story, at what point in your life would you begin the new chapter—and why? Journal your thoughts on this.

• • •

Alright, that's the Majors. Now let's move on to the Minor Arcana.

The Minor Arcana

The Minor Arcana are associated with the day-to-day events and things we have some control over: our jobs, relationships, money, and conflicts.

There are four suits in the Minors:

Wands: Fire element, work, passion, creativity

Cups: Water element, emotions, relationships, intuition

Swords: Air element, thoughts, conflicts

Pentacles: Earth element, money, material possessions, values

Within the Minors, there are four Courts for each suit:

Pages: Young people, students, messages, seeds. Pages can also represent the beginning of a new understanding. Perhaps you are starting to take the first steps on a journey or are just becoming aware of the present moment and future possibilities. You're green but ready to go forth and see what you might discover. This is the pivotal moment when you choose to start fresh.

Knights: Young people who identify as males, actions. Knights are moving past the first steps and are starting to make their mark in the world. This is an exciting time on your journey, where you are eager to take action and have new adventures. But you must be careful. Although you have more tools at your disposal, you have not yet acquired the wisdom you need. So keep your armor on and stay alert.

Queens: Mature people who identify as female and nurturing. Now you're acquiring fundamental, solid skills. You know who you are and how to manage your kingdom. This period is fertile, creative, and ripe. You are better able to understand your journey and yourself. This marks a period when you nurture your goals as you continue to grow. You know what needs to be done and how to do it.

Kings: Mature people who identify as male, mastery. Kings represent maturity, the culmination of a long journey. You have the experience, wisdom, and tools you need. You've completed your mission and can make informed decisions. Now you can take charge, stand in your power, and lead.

The Court cards can be tricky to interpret. Much will depend on the context of the question. If there are many Court cards in the reading, that is a sign the situation will be affected by many other people.

Keep in mind that you can be any one of the Courts. Do not get hung up on gender or age. For example, when taking a class, I would be a Page even though I identify as a Queen most of the time.

The Courts can represent different aspects of ourselves at various times in our life . . . or spiritual growth. They can indicate how we are maturing, not just emotionally but also spiritually. Each Court gives us different lessons and experiences. After you move through those situations, you have new tools to help you on your journey.

Practice: Take all of the Court cards out of your deck. Then begin associating each Court member with a different time in your life when you've played that role. For example, you might choose the Page of Swords to represent your high school years or the Queen of Pentacles for a time when you received a promotion. Have fun with this!

The Numbers

Except for the Court cards, every Minor is numbered from 1 to 10. These numbers have meanings and can provide insight into our journey.

Aces: Aces are associated with the number 1 and signify a new beginning. You'll notice each card features a hand coming out of a cloud holding one of the suits: Wand, Cup, Sword, or Pentacle. This image could be viewed as an offering or gift. The cloud obscures part of the hand, which means the journey is only at the beginning; it's hard to see where it will end. But now you're ready to go—and grow. In Tarot Wisdom, Rachel Pollack says: "These symbolize divine grace, the idea that the power of the suit just comes to us at this moment in our lives."

Two: Twos symbolize choices. Now you must consider which direction you will take. There may be opportunities or options. Which way will you go? The next step is up to you. Twos are also associated with duality. Finding the balance between two opposing forces can feel challenging, but unity is possible after you figure out how to go with the flow.

Three: Three is the number of creativity. You can create something entirely new. What will that be? Something is being born or transformed. The energy is rich, fertile, and full of possibilities. This could mark the arrival of a catalyst, which triggers growth.

Four: Four is associated with stability and order. Everything falls into a rhythm. You can achieve security at this time. The Fours show a rest period when you can dream of new possibilities. This number is also associated with building a foundation.

Five: Five is considered a challenging number because it represents change. It's the midpoint of the numbers and symbolizes a crossroad. You can see whether what you've built is sturdy . . . or not. A struggle may arise, external or internal. However, within that conflict lies an opportunity for new growth.

Six: Sixes mean balance and harmony. After the disruptive Five, this number promises peace will return. You can complete the necessary work and find equilibrium. You have what you need and can be generous with others. This is a sentimental card, also associated with giving or support.

Seven: Once again, a challenge emerges with the number Seven. Just when you think the dust has settled, a new obstacle or test is on the way. Your mettle will be tested; you must persevere. This is the moment in your journey when you feel overwhelmed, but if you press on, you will experience a breakthrough.

Eight: Eight symbolizes success and completion. You overcame the issues and are getting your priorities in divine order. The hard work has paid off with renewed confidence, rewards, and fresh options. Where will you go from here?

Nine: Nine is associated with completion, material success, and contentment. You've achieved so much—and should feel fulfilled. A new phase is on the way, but first, stop and enjoy what you've created. Find meaning in the present before you move on to the next thing. Nines also amplify the energy of the suit, which can mean the most intense expression.

Ten: Tens are endings with a new beginning all wrapped up in one. This marks the culmination of all your efforts and lessons. What wisdom have you gained, and what will you carry into the next cycle?

👁 **Pro tip:** When you are doing a reading, notice if there are multiple cards with the same number. This is an important clue as to what is happening in the querent's life. For example, if all of the Fives show up, this is an alert they may be going through a tumultuous time. I've also found it's helpful to point this out to the querent. Oftentimes, they will have a story to tell about what's going on!

• • •

Now we're ready to explore the Minors.

Ace of Wands

A new beginning is possible. The Ace of Wands signals a rebirth, a chance to start anew. No matter what you've been through, you are ready to rise up from the ashes and soar again like a phoenix. Let the past go and embrace the new life right in front of you. The Ace of Wands can also symbolize an offer: this can be a job, creative project, or a helping hand. It can also mean a new treatment. Whatever is being offered seems like a "yes." Recovery. Getting your fire back. Searching for meaning. Beginning a new cycle of spiritual development or self-awareness. The catalyst for change. The first spark of creativity.

Reversed: Your energy is lagging, and you need to rest. Although you have things to do, sometimes those things can wait. Come back to them when you feel up to it. If you have trouble asking for help, this card says: reach out. You'll get the support you need if you do. It's also possible you may be trying to help someone, but they refuse. Lastly, if you feel called to extend an olive branch to someone you've wronged, it's never too late. An inability to trust yourself. A lack of courage. Starting something but running out of gas. Erection issues.

Journaling prompt: What are some new paths I could try?

Two of Wands

Everything is going according to plan. You can see results. Keep doing what you're doing because it is working. If you want to explore new options, that's fine too. Sometimes it's good to have more support or choices. Travel may be necessary at this time. Perhaps you're visiting a loved one or going away for a sabbatical. This card can also symbolize an expert. The Two of Wands can mean staying home until things settle down too. Prepping for a new journey. There are many options and possibilities to consider at this time. Evaluate your progress and reflect on your current situation as well as past successes. You can build self-confidence now. Complete your work. Do not just dream of what's possible; make it happen.

Reversed: Things begin to stall out. Progress is lost. This situation could be frustrating. You will need to be patient at this time. Or you might have to try a different option. What sort of plan B do you have in place? Inability to travel. Being stuck at home. Forced to wait it out. Dissatisfaction. Spiritual stagnation. You cannot put plans into action. Stalemate. Living in a fantasy world. Refusing to accept reality or to interact with the world at large. A recluse or shut-in. Watching the world pass you by.

Journaling prompt: What options have I not explored?

Three of Wands

There is a light at the end of the tunnel. You're over the hump and on your way. New options are available soon. You can try new things and see where they take you. If you're looking for a new job or place to live, this card is favorable. You can see clearly now, and life is looking up. Success after a long journey. The beginning of something amazing. Acknowledge how far you've come while remaining open to new possibilities. Explore. Seek and accept help. You don't need to go it alone. Help is on the horizon. You may need to make a move soon. Do not be intimidated by limitations. You can move beyond them. Adjust your plans accordingly.

Reversed: Plans are falling apart. A complication arises, and now you have to retreat. Maybe your plan wasn't strong to begin with. Or perhaps a complication threw everything off. Either way, step back, rest up, and look at where you can go from here. Sometimes this card can indicate getting ill on a trip (Montezuma's revenge!). An inability to see the bigger picture. An unrealistic attitude. Staying close to home or the failure to appreciate what is close at hand. An unwillingness to try new things. Refusing help. Going it alone. Turning your back on the world. Looking within rather than outside yourself.

Journaling prompt: When I think of the future, how do I feel?

Four of Wands

A celebration is in order. You receive good news or someone close to you does. Be ready to break out the cake and toss the confetti! A feeling of optimism is in the air. Life is better, and the hard work has paid off. This can also mean a visit from the family, or spending time in the country. A weekend away could do the mind, body, and soul good. This could also represent a healing center. Celebrating the completion of a successful endeavor or journey. You've won! Acknowledge your success. Acknowledge your team for all their help. Celebrate life!

Reversed: Four of Wands reversed is still a good card, but the joy is cautiously optimistic. Instead of whooping it up, you're still crossing your fingers and holding your breath. A mini celebration. An unexpected visit from the family. Health improves bit by bit. Returning home after a period of being away. Not allowing yourself to experience joy. Never feeling as though it's enough or complete.

Journaling prompt: When do I most feel at home?

Five of Wands

A struggle. This is not the time to give up. Instead, you must fight. The situation may feel scary at first, but soon you'll be energized. Confront your obstacles head on. A difference of opinions. Maybe you don't like what you're hearing. It's okay to push back. Be an advocate for yourself and explore other options. A power play. Family drama. The struggle between inner and outer growth. Inner chaos.

Reversed: The struggle comes to an end. You can let go. There is no need to keep on fighting. It's not worth your time. Advice coming from a team of legal experts. Hustling to reach a goal. Internalized stress. Fighting a cold, infection, or virus. Low energy.

Assuming you can do this alone. Refusing to listen to another point of view. Giving up. Following the wrong leader. Getting lost in the shuffle.

Journaling prompt: In what way am I fighting for myself . . . or need to?

Six of Wands

The Six of Wands is one of the best cards to see in a reading about health. It means victory or a healing. You come to the end of a journey with flying colors. Success at last. A support team is by your side. Good news. You're riding high. The Six of Wands can also indicate taking the lead in a situation. Others may depend on you now, and you won't let them down. If you're put in charge, you will do the right thing. The future looks optimistic. You're going in the right direction. You're in harmony with your surroundings. All is well. Taking the high road.

Reversed: Small gains. You're making progress, but it's slow going. A setback. Lacking support, you may feel alone in your situation. Bad leadership or professionals who don't live up to their reputation. Accidents. Uncertainty about where you're going from here. Impulsiveness. Don't rush to the finish line. Things are taking time. Deceit and betrayal. A lack of confidence in yourself or others. Feeling blue. Getting on your high horse and acting like a blowhard.

Journaling prompt: Where could more support make a difference?

Seven of Wands

Fighting or facing a situation with courage. You've got a big battle ahead and may feel outnumbered, but still you will prevail. Take one day at a time, rise to every challenge, and keep fighting. Before long, you'll see you can do this. You might feel as if you're on your own at this time. Everything is coming at you all at once. Stress. Or you're waking up to a new reality. A change is happening. Find a way to work with this change, even if it feels difficult. Setting boundaries. Enough is enough. It's time to protect your energy or body. Sometimes this card means getting back on your feet again. Take a small action; this will restore your sense of self.

Reversed: The battle comes to an end. You finish the job or decide to let go. No defenses. You're unprepared to handle your challenges. Losing courage. It's too much for you. This may be the time to ask for help rather than going it alone. Walking away and resting. Sometimes this reversal means getting everything in order. Giving in to the wishes of others even though you know it's not the best. Not standing up for yourself. Letting others push you around. Feeling overwhelmed because you took on too much.

Journaling prompt: How can I do my part without becoming overwhelmed?

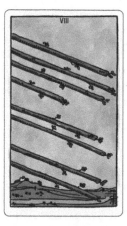

Eight of Wands

Good news comes in. Everything is moving in the right direction. A healing is on the way. More energy. Situations are changing rapidly, and you have to adjust. Travel by air— perhaps to visit family. A long overdue and much deserved vacation. Feeling enthusiastic for the future. A situation may be "up in the air." There are no clear answers, but news is coming in rapidly. The situation may be changing minute by minute. Slow down and give yourself room to evaluate what is happening. Avoid making decisions in the moment until things settle down.

Reversed: New problems enter the situation. A complication puts a wrinkle in your progress. You may need to take a detour. A lack of courage because you're not seeing results. Retreat. Giving up—or rushing into a new situation without any forethought. Unhappy news. Ignoring a situation when you probably need to take control of it. Lack of energy. Putting off taking action. Plans that go nowhere fast.

Journaling prompt: Where are things going?

Nine of Wands

Just when you thought you were out of the woods, a setback occurs. Now you have to go back to the drawing board and perhaps start from the beginning. Strength in the midst of battle. Paranoia. Fear. You don't trust the experts or your team. Isolated and having to do all the work alone. Setting boundaries. Feeling wounded by a situation or person. Quarantine. Protection. You will find your way. Facing the past and learning from it. The wounded warrior. Preparing to do battle. Make time for healing before making a final decision.

Reversed: You can drop your defenses. The situation seems to be resolving itself. Help arrives, and you're no longer on your own. Let down your guard and allow other people to help. Forgiveness. A healing. The old wound is mended. Or a health issue that doesn't seem to be going away (for example, a chronic condition). Feeling immobilized by fear or doubt. Trying to ignore the past—or getting stuck there and unable to be in the present moment. Buried issues that cause pain. Or wanting to live in the past because you assume those were the good old days. Refusing to make amends. Becoming immobilized by fear or doubt.

Journaling prompt: What wound needs tending?

Ten of Wands

Heavy responsibilities. You're carrying the weight of the world on your shoulders. Not enough support. Everything and everyone feels like a burden. Someone is "on your back." In questions about addiction, this is the monkey on your back. Weighed down. An obstacle you didn't see coming. You're in the final leg of a hard journey. This is your breaking point, but you must persevere toward your goal, no matter how hard it seems. Remain focused on the outcome you want. Keep going. You know where you're going and shouldn't give up. Have you taken on more than you can handle? Sometimes this card can indicate back trouble or hard labor.

Reversed: The burden lifts. Help arrives at last. You're no longer on your own. This could be the end of a situation. Something finally gives. Or you're getting out from under a responsibility. An ending. You're free at last! Sometimes this card can indicate an unwillingness to face a situation. So you put your head down and ignore what's right in front of your face. Procrastinating today what you can put off tomorrow. A refusal to set priorities. Fobbing the responsibility off on someone else's shoulders. Saying no to help.

Journaling prompt: What's weighing me down at this moment?

Page of Wands

The Page of Wands symbolizes a fresh start. You have a chance to follow your passions or to begin a new spiritual journey. A risk may be involved, but do not let that hold you back. Instead, go in with an open mind, take that first step, and see what unfolds. It could be a grand adventure! Pages can signal important news too. Perhaps you or someone you know has an exciting announcement! In a reading, the Page of Wands could also represent an enthusiastic young person. For a health question, this card could symbolize the beginning of a healthier period.

Reversed: Restless, reckless behavior. You're taking risks without guarantees, safety nets, or regard for other people. Or maybe you refuse to take a leap of faith, and instead choose an easy, familiar route. Another way to look at this reversal is indecision. Perhaps you're unsure what to do, or fear is clouding your judgement. It can also mean bad news. This reversal can also symbolize a rebellious young person who refuses to follow the rules.

Journaling prompt: What new things am I willing to explore?

Knight of Wands

A busy period with a lot of coming and going. You're fired up and raring to go! Not much can stop you now. You have more energy than usual and are not afraid to go where you've never gone before. Charge forward and see where the road takes you. This could be a time with new opportunities, challenges, or freedom. You can inspire others through your courage. You'll need to act quickly because the fire may burn out as fast as it ignites. The Knight of Wands can symbolize a young person who brings excitement into the situation or a rescuer. Their bravery could get you through a scary time. Sometimes this card can mean a new path, treatment, or passion.

Reversed: You're doing what you want without considering possible consequences. This selfish behavior could get someone hurt—including yourself. It's also possible you feel inflamed, or the fire is out. This reversal can also mean you're forced to slow down. Maybe you're unwell, or other circumstances are creating obstacles. The Knight of Wands reversed can represent a hot-tempered person or a bully. Depression. You feel lazy and uninspired and just wish someone else would take the reins.

Journaling prompt: What risks might be worth it?

QUEEN OF WANDS.

Queen of Wands

This proud Queen says: you are sitting in a place of authority. Be confident and approach every issue with bravery. There may be a situation or two where you must take a bold stance. You are aware of the power you possess, and you wield it fairly. You protect your hearth and home, and you're an advocate for yourself or other people. The Queen of Wands nurtures their loved ones and creative fire while tending to their own inner flame. This card can symbolize a passionate person who has a magnetic and generous personality. They create beauty wherever they go.

Reversed: Your flame is burning low. You may be overdoing it or lacking confidence. Obstacles or too many responsibilities have affected your well-being. You need to step back and care for yourself. Or maybe you're caring for others and need to forgo your needs to ensure they get what they need first. The sacrifices are great. This reversal could also symbolize a time when nothing seems to be going the way you want. You're forced to sit there and wait it out. The Queen of Wands reversed can also represent a selfish or weak-willed person with no connection to their spiritual life.

Journaling prompt: Where do you need more courage?

KING OF WANDS.

King of Wands

The King of Wands indicates you have control of the situation. You know what you're doing and when to act. Trust your instincts, for they will serve you well. You can inspire others with your fiery, enthusiastic manner if you're in a leadership role. You are a role model of spiritual strength and power. People love being around you because you motivate them to do better. However, it can also mean a time when you must take a calculated risk. This card can represent a mentor, coach, or open-minded health-care practitioner. It's also associated with creativity. Where will your imagination take you next? Let it run wild!

Reversed: You think you know what's best . . . when maybe you don't. Or perhaps you're afraid to follow your instincts, so you go along with the experts, even when you don't want to. The King of Wands reversed is like the cowardly lion—unable to stand up for themselves or letting pride get in the way. Sometimes this card can represent a reckless authority figure or wannabe dictator. Instead of inspiring, they use fear to control others. If this card shows up, you'll want to keep your temper in check.

Journaling prompt: When do I act on my instincts, and when do I ignore them?

Practice: The Wands suit is associated with creativity. Think of it like this: they are the Fire element, the spark of inspiration that leads to new ideas. The next time you find yourself stuck on a problem or an "old story," take the Wands out of your deck. Shuffle them up and choose one or more. Use these cards as a prompt to ponder solutions or to uncover a new narrative. For example, say you feel ashamed for something you did eons ago. That's a storyline that could keep you from moving forward. Using this exercise, you might pull the Two of Wands, Ten of Wands, and Queen of Wands reversed. The new story could go something like this: "I've gone through a situation and survived. I did the best I could. I'm ready to release this burden of shame. As I release the past, I feel calm and cool . . . and wiser."

Pro tip: In a Tarot reading about grief, loss, or illness, it may seem weird when people want to ask about mundane things such as work. Keep in mind that a job can feel like an anchor during hard times. For example, my family tends to throw themselves into work when life is challenging. It's partially a way to escape, but also an opportunity to contribute something meaningful even if we feel unwell or sad. I like to say that work is our therapy!

Ace of Cups

The beginning of a happy period. You're feeling good, inside and out. Everything seems to be flowing in the right direction. The Ace of Cups indicates you can express your emotions freely. Nothing is holding you back. This card can also mean a new cycle of self-love or improved emotional health. It's also associated with renewal, rebirth, birth, or conception. Sometimes it suggests an offer or a helping hand when you need it most. A message from Spirit or a gift. Be receptive . . . and ready to give back. The Holy Grail.

Reversed: Emotions are getting in the way. They are overflowing, or you're depleted from a challenging situation. You need more time to rest and "refill your cup." Sometimes this card can mean pushing people away or refusing to acknowledge how you feel. In those cases, you could be harming yourself. It's also possible that help offered is withdrawn. The Ace of Cups reversed can mean being hung up on the past or unable to see the abundance life offers you. In some cases, this can indicate fertility issues. Lastly, are you saying no when you mean yes, or vice versa?

Journaling prompt: What do I need to receive right now?

Two of Cups

The Two of Cups is one of the best cards to see in a reading about health. The symbol between the two figures shows healing is taking place. It's the power of love to heal all or having the right support when you need it most. This card can indicate a willingness to meet other folks halfway or coming together in the spirit of love. Unity. You're making good, heart-centered decisions. Sometimes this means getting a second opinion. A divine connection between two people.

Reversed: Feeling unwell or unbalanced. You're overwhelmed and not supported. Or a relationship falls apart when you need it most. Maybe they pull away . . . or you're pushing them away. The Two of Cups can mean a disappointment after a period when things were looking up. I've also seen this card mean a guilt trip or manipulation.

Journaling prompt: What needs to be healed at this time?

Three of Cups

The Three of Cups means happy news arrives, and you have a reason to celebrate! Things are looking up at last! All that hard work has paid off, and it's time to party! This card can also represent a supportive circle of friends or loved ones rallying around you when you need them most. For some, it can symbolize a support group, coven, or another type of network. A pregnancy or baby shower. It's also possible you're rejoicing in someone else's success. Life is good!

Reversed: This reversal can represent a premature celebration. Things are not where they need to be just yet. You must wait a bit longer. It can also mean wishing things were different or being unwilling to celebrate other people's good fortune. For some, this is "falling off the wagon" or a relapse. I've also seen this card mean a sad gathering.

Journaling prompt: How can I find pleasure at this moment?

Four of Cups

The Four of Cups indicates low energy. You may feel slug-gish or tired. Or maybe you've run out of steam and just don't care anymore. If this is the case, rest may be neces-sary. This could also mean rejecting an offer or not liking the options in front of you. Or perhaps you're disgusted with the help you're getting or not getting. Maybe you feel isolated . . . or choose to be. I've also seen this card mean rejecting a situation or going along with it reluctantly. In some cases, this card can say: don't give up; new options are on the way. For spiritual questions, meditation or time in a sanctuary could restore your spirit. Your higher purpose is revealed, or your guides are offering a solution. Pay attention, or you will miss the memo.

Reversed: You may be examining a new set of options. Or maybe further help is available. A solution seems to arrive out of thin air. A few missteps may reveal the correct answer. It's also possible you're returning to the swing of things after a time out. You can establish new routines at last. I've also seen this reversal mean quarantine or an enforced period of being in solitude. The reversed Four of Cups can also suggest you need to acknowledge other people's input. If you ignore what is being presented, you may regret it later.

Journaling prompt: Why am I not feeling this?

Five of Cups

The Five of Cups is the classic card of mourning. You're deep in grief and not ready to move on yet. You must go through the process at your own pace. What's important is that you honor your feelings and take your time. Even though there is a loss, there are still things left standing. You can pick up those pieces when you're ready and start over. Sometimes the Five of Cups means you feel alone or depressed. If so, it may be time to ask for help. In some cases, this card is associated with escapism through substances. You don't want to face what's happening, so you drown your sorrows. It's also possible you are letting old issues and failures impact your present happiness. Just remember, what seems like a failure may be an overlooked opportunity.

Reversed: You're in recovery at last. Now you can begin rebuilding your life. You are moving past grief and into the future. Feeling hopeful again. In some cases, this reversal could mean pretending like everything is okay when it's not. If that is happening, you must be honest with your loved ones. They cannot help you if you aren't willing to admit what is going on. Or maybe you're wallowing in negative emotions or feeling like a victim. This card can represent a grief counselor.

Journaling prompt: How can I best honor the hard feelings?

Six of Cups

This sweet card is associated with finding pleasure in the past . . . or going back to make amends. You're ready to extend the olive branch or forgive. This is a time when your perspective is wiser. You can understand how past deeds led to the present situation. The Six of Cups can also mean a visit from an old friend. In some cases, this card can mean receiving good news or gifts. Or you're making a decision that promotes harmony and healing. It's also associated with children. This could mean issues centered around children's needs or you're making peace with your childhood. How has your childhood shaped who you became today, and how will you nurture your inner child? For a reading about deceased folks, this card shows spirits returning to their childhood home. It can also mean receiving a message from a departed loved one.

Reversed: You're letting go of the past . . . or clinging to it. Depending on the question, you could be trapped in the good old days or desperately trying to forget about them. It can also mean making peace with someone from back in the day. I've also seen this reversal indicate old issues returning to haunt someone. Sometimes the Six of Cups reversed says you're burned out from giving too much. Or you're fearful of new challenges, so you stay in the comfort zone hoping for a miracle with no effort. This can indicate a longing to connect with folks who passed on in mediumship readings.

Journaling prompt: What can I learn from the past?

Seven of Cups

You have many options before you. Choose carefully. Be sure to explore every single one in depth because more than one path could work now. You might be able to combine more than one modality at the same time. The other side of this card is an imagination running wild. Are you dreaming of the future? Wanting to be somewhere else? Or is your head lost in the clouds? You'll want to watch out for wishful thinking or an unrealistic attitude. While having a strong imagination is excellent, you don't want to let it run away from you. Sometimes this card can mean dream work or a shift in your spiritual development. Suddenly, you see a new way of connecting with something greater than yourself.

Reversed: This reversal indicates a reality check. You must face what's happening, whether you like it or not. There is no getting around it. It's also possible a choice is being made for you, or maybe you are the one making a decision for someone else. The Seven of Cups reversed can mean hypochondria or imagining a worst-case scenario. If you're making assumptions, you might be wiser to consult a professional rather than attempt to diagnose yourself. In a mediumship reading, it can mean confusing messages from the beyond.

Journaling prompt: How can I gather more information about my current choices?

Eight of Cups

You are moving on. What's done is done; don't look back. Instead, you must look ahead. There may be a whole new life waiting for you. You won't know unless you go. The Eight of Cups can represent a physical or spiritual journey. It can also symbolize time spent in a retreat or recovery. Maybe you're getting sober or finding your purpose. Soul-searching can lead you to the answer you seek. This card can also mean detaching from the world or a situation. You're leaving it all behind. Sometimes this card is about becoming your own guide. You're moving into the Hermit's realm and finding your inner wisdom.

Reversed: Now you're coming back to a situation after a time out. Maybe you're returning from vacation or time spent in seclusion. Or perhaps you're coming home from the hospital. Either way, you're ready to go back to your nest. The other side of this reversal is the inability to move on. Instead, you keep going back to your comfort zone. That could mean repeating old mistakes, falling off the wagon, or staying in situations you've outgrown. Sometimes, this reversal could mean someone is coming back into your life.

Journaling prompt: Where do I go from here?

Nine of Cups

The Nine of Cups is one of the "wish" cards in the Tarot, so it's always a welcome card to see. A wish is fulfilled, intentions manifested, and miracles have happened. Everything is falling into divine order. At last, you're getting to your happy place. This card also means good health; however, it can point to indulgence or overdoing the "good life." Celebrate your wins but know your limits. The Nine of Cups can also indicate a time when you have everything and everyone stacked in your favor. The odds are good, and you can enjoy the fruits of your labor.

Reversed: You're not getting what you want at this time. Your wishes are delayed or simply not granted. This sucks, but perhaps there is a good reason for it. Sometimes we get what we need, not what we desire. The Nine of Cups reversed can also mean laziness, sloth, or greed. You're acting entitled and as if the world owes you a favor. In some readings, this card can indicate addiction or relapse.

Journaling prompt: What do I want the most?

Ten of Cups

At last, the happy ending. Everything comes together in the best way possible. You return home or experience complete healing. The support you need is by your side. This is the rainbow after the storm, the moment when you can feel good about the future once again. It can also mean you're lending support to someone else. Maybe you're taking care of the family or holding down the fort while someone else is away. All in all, the best possible outcome is on the way. Your dreams are coming to fruition. Now you can share in your happiness and good fortune. This card can also mean joining a new community. In a mediumship reading, this shows a welcoming committee on the other side.

Reversed: You're leaving home. You might be returning to the hospital or walking away because the family dynamics have become toxic. If you don't have support from them, why bother? You're also possibly fighting with loved ones over a legacy or caregiving duties. Or maybe you're ignoring the needs of others around you. This card can indicate a time when you have no resources and must rely on the kindness of strangers. In some cases, you cannot see the joy around you.

Journaling prompt: What would make my life feel harmonious at this moment?

PAGE OF CUPS.

Page of Cups

The Page of Cups heralds a positive message. You're getting the news your heart desires. This message could be something you're anticipating or a complete surprise. Sometimes the message could be from the other side too. It could mean the beginning of emotional healing or transformation. You're learning how to share your feelings in a whole new way. It's also possible this card could indicate healing the inner child or dealing with children's issues. In some cases, this card can mean feeling loved or needed. Lastly, if you need to make a decision, this Page says: follow your heart.

Reversed: You receive a message that causes emotional stress. Or you're unable to face reality, so you act like a spoiled child. Immaturity or naivety. This reversal could mean you desire a change but haven't bothered to consider what that might entail. Another interpretation could be concern over a young person. If a child is going through a tough time, they may be on your mind. The other side of this card is a family member withdrawing their support. They no longer want to help out.

Journaling prompt: What does my heart have to say about my current situation?

KNIGHT OF CUPS.

Knight of Cups

Your feelings are telling you exactly where you need to go from here. You must listen to your heart even if it doesn't make sense. This is your intuition at work. The Knight of Cups can mean an offer of love or support. Someone is ready to lend a hand, or maybe you're the one making the gesture. This card can represent a healer or rescuer. It's the person you can count on when life feels challenging. They'll be there in any way you need. However, this Knight can be moody. When they feel triggered, watch out!

Reversed: You're emotionally all over the place. You are scattered with no grounding. Instead, you drift through a situation without rhyme, reason, or commitment. Or maybe you've given up. Instead of doing the work, you've found the escape hatch. This card can sometimes indicate addiction, or a physical situation made worse by emotional instability. The Knight of Cups reversed can also mean losing objectivity. Perhaps you've become too emotionally involved in a situation, or maybe someone is gaslighting you. This card can also represent a con artist who uses feelings to manipulate others.

Journaling prompt: Where are my feelings leading me?

QUEEN OF CUPS.

Queen of Cups

The Queen of Cups is deeply in touch with her emotions and intuition. She's highly psychic, so if this card represents you, you must pay close attention to your gut. Allow your feelings to guide you. Sensitivity is high at this time. Your emotions run deep but can quickly turn stormy. You'll need to take care they don't overwhelm you at times. This card can represent an empath, therapist, caregiver, or gifted healer. They provide the right kind of emotional support. If you're playing that role, your nurturing could be comforting.

Reversed: You can't see straight. Your emotions are blinding you at this time. Or you can't get in touch with them; you turned them off. If this is the case, you'll want to refrain from making decisions until you are balanced. Sometimes this reversal indicates a pity party. In that case, you're in full-blown martyr mode. You feel sorry for yourself and are unable to move on. It's also possible you're grief-stricken. In that case, you may need help to recover. The Queen of Cups reversed can signal a time when you lose touch with reality. This card can also represent active addiction or codependency. Toxic positivity is another interpretation.

Journaling prompt: How can I better express what I feel?

KING OF CUPS.

King of Cups

Emotional maturity. You are facing a situation with courage. Now you can see through the problems with creative solutions. You can find the balance between sensitive and stoic, no matter how tough things are. This card can represent a caregiver, loving healer, or counselor. They provide the kind of support that makes you feel safe. Sometimes the King of Cups means mastering your emotions or yourself. You know who you are and take responsibility for yourself. Other possible interpretations are expressing your feelings with power or taking the lead in delicate situations.

Reversed: You've lost your nerve. Your emotions got the best of you, and now you're too scared to take action or express how you feel. Or you turn off your feelings because you don't want to face the music. Like an ostrich, you've buried your head in the sand. If you're pretending it's okay when it's not, the truth will hit you in the face at some point. The King of Cups reversed can also mean drowning your sorrows or refusing to accept help. In some cases, this card represents a dishonest person who uses emotional blackmail to meet their needs.

Journaling prompt: What is the kindest and most courageous thing I can do right now?

Practice: The Cups suit speaks to our emotions and is the perfect suit for journaling. One of my favorite ways to journal is "art journaling," which I find to be therapeutic and fun, especially when I'm in a funk. Here's what to do: pull a card from the Cups suit that best symbolizes how you feel. This card will be your inspiration. You can choose to paint, draw, or paste clippings from magazines that represent that card. If you like, you can mix mediums too. (My favorite: I have been making tiny cartoon diaries in wee journals. This has been a joyful practice; plus, it's fun to revisit my cartooning skills!)

Pro tip: Cups cards can reveal a lot about how much support a querent has . . . or needs. Pay close attention to cards such as the Five of Cups or any of the reversed Courts in this suit. These cards can indicate they are struggling. Also, sometimes folks aren't able to articulate how they feel or what they need. A Tarot reading could open the door to a much-needed conversation. I recommend pointing to any concerning cards and asking the querent, "How does this card make you feel?" Then give them the floor.

Ace of Swords

A mental breakthrough. The clouds part, and you can see what's really going on. The aha moment arrives at last! A new solution to an old problem has been discovered. The Ace of Swords can also mean severing ties. Perhaps someone has crossed a line, and now you need to create boundaries. Doing so will help you take back your power. This card can also indicate a new way of thinking. Maybe you're starting school or eliminating old beliefs. Keep in mind that Swords are also associated with conflict. That means this could be the start of a battle. In a health reading, this card can symbolize a new treatment or a surgery.

Reversed: An aggressive attitude could lead to injury. It would be best if you watched that your words or actions do not cause harm. Of course, this card can also mean mental stress or creative blocks. You cannot see the forest through the trees or are unable to proceed. In some readings, this reversal means putting down the sword and refusing to fight. You've given up or are too scared to make a move. It's also possible you're unable to think clearly at this time. Your head is stuck in the clouds.

Journaling prompt: What is the point I'm trying to make?

Two of Swords

You must sit tight and weigh your options. Nothing is clear at this time. In fact, both sides may have merit. Therefore, you do not want to rush to make a decision. Instead, you'll need to gather the facts or get a second opinion. This card can mean quarantine, recovery time, or eye troubles in health readings. The blindfold symbolizes an unwillingness to face the truth as well. In that case, you close yourself off. The Two of Swords can also mean making peace with your situation. You've come to terms.

Reversed: The Two of Swords reversed means getting back in the game after time away. Life becomes busy, but you feel energized! This can also mean seeing the light. The blind-fold comes off, and the truth is plain to see. In some cases, this reversal could indicate losing your sense of balance. If you took on too many responsibilities, something needs to give. I've also seen this reversal mean getting stuck in the middle of a feud with no easy way out.

Journaling prompt: What do I need to see?

Three of Swords

Loss, grief, depression, heartbreak. An old wound is reopened, or a new one is formed. This card symbolizes pain—both physical and emotional. The heart is torn into pieces, a sign that something has come to an irrevocable end. There is no turning back because the damage is too significant. You're forced to move on. Sometimes the Three of Swords means betrayal. Other times, it's a reve-lation that gets to the heart of the matter. It can also indi-cate a turbulent period. Whatever has happened, make time for grief, but watch that you don't get stuck there.

Reversed: The healing is beginning at last. Finally, a storm has passed, and clarity arrives. You're feeling much better. Maybe you're coming through an emotional situation or recovering from surgery. Whatever the case, the Three of Swords is the light at the end of a long, dark tunnel. You can begin to move on. Relief is in sight. This card can also mean making peace after a feud.

Journaling prompt: What is my pain trying to tell me?

Four of Swords

The Four of Swords card is often associated with healing, respite, and recovery. It's the rest period after a battle, such as a leave of absence. You may be spending time in retreat or reflection. Or maybe you are in quarantine, separated from the outside world. Whatever the case, this will allow you to get back on your feet. It can symbolize a hospital, ashram, or rehab center. You might be spending time in such a place or visiting a loved one. The Four of Swords can also mean sleeping on a decision or making plans for the future. You need a sabbatical to think things over. It can also mean coming to terms or making peace with a situation.

Reversed: You're back in action. At last you are recovered and feel much better. You've done the work to heal yourself and can continue your usual routine. Sometimes the Four of Swords can mean leaving the hospital or rehab. But it can also say you cannot get the rest you need to heal. In that case, this could be a nudge to schedule time for recuperation. This card can symbolize a memorial service or funeral planning as well.

Journaling prompt: How much rest do I need?

Five of Swords

The Five of Swords is a card of conflict. Perhaps the family is at odds over a loved one's care. Or a war begins because someone doesn't want to accept responsibility for the pain they caused. Everything turns stormy, and feelings are hurt. It's also possible someone uses deceptive means to gain control of a situation. They are not telling the whole story because they want an unfair advantage or to lord their power over others. This is the win at all costs, no matter who gets harmed. When the Five of Swords arrives, it can also be a warning to not turn your back on someone.

Reversed: Lies come out into the open. Now the truth is revealed. There may still be grief and pain, but at least the conflict is at an end. You may have regrets over the way things went down. But you can put the past in the past and forgive. This could mark a period of healing old wrongs and making things right. Suppose you or the other people involved can take responsibility for your roles in the event. In that case, the conflict can end on a beautiful note.

Journaling prompt: What am I trying to get away with now?

Six of Swords

After the stormy energy of the Five of Swords, the Six of Swords shows people in a boat, moving on. This image signals a healing journey has begun. The support you need is by your side. No matter how rough things may seem, everything will start to smooth over soon. You must trust the bad times aren't forever. After all, nothing is ever permanent. The Six of Swords is a reminder that everything moves on eventually. You can leave the hard times behind and look ahead to calmer days. This card can also mark a transition to a new life or a gateway to a new perspective. Either way, you have much to look forward to. Trust the process.

The three figures also remind you that you're not alone. "We're in this boat together." Together, we can make a change.

Reversed: This reversal says you're unable to move on. Instead, you're stuck like a car in the snow, spinning its tires. There is little to no traction. Maybe you don't have the help you need. Or perhaps you've rejected that assistance and now must figure your own way out. Either way, nothing can change until you let go or ask for help. If you're holding on to something dearly, you cannot make room for anything new to grow. The reversed Six of Swords is the dark night of the soul, a difficult journey, and the moment when the old situation returns. For some, this card can mean returning to the hospital or rehab. It can also advise: don't rock the boat.

Journaling prompt: How can I best move on from this situation?

Seven of Swords

The Seven of Swords is a tricky card. On the one hand, it indicates deception. Conversely, it can show a need to fly under the radar to avoid drama. A third way of looking at it: getting away with something. No matter what is going on, there is a subterfuge taking place. You or someone involved in the situation may be resorting to deceit to reach a goal. Whether this is positive or negative will depend on the question. For example, if you're attempting to surprise a loved one, that's not bad. But sneaking around and lying to get your way isn't right. Sometimes the Seven of Swords symbolizes a daring feat. You pulled something off despite incredible odds. Or maybe you let a few things go to move a situation forward. In other cases, this card shows treachery or a bold theft. As I said, it's tricky.

Reversed: You're caught in the act instead of getting away with it. Or maybe you're returning to the situation because you forgot something and want to retrieve it. On the other hand, perhaps you just can't leave well enough alone. Either way, this reversal shows the plans are not working out, but soon you'll understand what went wrong. This is also a reminder to seek help instead of going it alone, especially if the situation is beyond your ability to handle it alone.

Journaling prompt: Where am I deceiving myself?

Eight of Swords

After the shifty Seven of Swords, on Eight of Swords we see a figure tied up and blindfolded. This card symbolizes a time when you cannot make a move. You feel helpless, stuck, or blocked. But how did this happen? There are no other figures in the card, a sign you got yourself in this position. Now you are forced to wait it out. Going within is the best way to see your way out of the situation. When you stop struggling and accept things, you'll know how you got here . . . and how to extricate yourself. You have agency, even though you may not be aware of it yet. The Eight of Swords can also mean feeling ostracized. Maybe you're allowing other people to control you. No one has the power to dictate how you should behave or think unless you let them. This card can also mean staying in your comfort zone, even if it does nothing to help you grow. In some cases, this card can indicate quarantine.

Reversed: You are free! At last, you've found your way out of the situation. Or something has changed. Fate intervened, and the binds were removed. Nothing can limit you now. The restrictions have been lifted, and you can move on. No matter how long you've been stuck, you finally figured out how to release yourself. You aced the test! The Eight of Swords reversed signals more breathing room and the ability to see things as they are.

Journaling prompt: How am I trapping myself?

Nine of Swords

Worries plague you. You cannot seem to escape your troubles. Instead, the Nine of Swords represents a time when you are filled with anxiety as you wait for the other shoe to drop. If you've been going through a trial, your fear may be clouding your judgement. However, you are not powerless, even though you might assume there is nothing you can do to change your situation. Help is available, but you must be willing to humble yourself and ask for it. You do not need to suffer in silence. In fact, you don't need to suffer at all. This card can also mean nightmares, depression, grief, and the dark night of the soul. It's a signal that situations are getting under your skin. But do know you are protected, and this too shall pass.

Reversed: At last, the nightmare comes to an end. Your pain is over. Now you have the support you need, which will help you move on. The Nine of Swords reversed is the light at the end of a long, dark tunnel. Instead of despair, you can find hope once again. This reversal can also symbolize coming out of the hospital or rehab. It can also mean receiving effective therapy. However, a negative reading can suggest you're repeating the same thing that brought you problems in the first place. If you haven't learned your lesson, soon you'll have a chance to repeat the experience.

Journaling prompt: What is the one fear I need to face now?

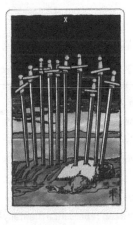

Ten of Swords

The Ten of Swords shows a figure facedown on the earth with swords in their back. A sunrise or sunset is on the horizon. This image symbolizes a complete ending with a change just over the horizon. Whatever has caused you pain is over. You can let go, remove those swords, and begin again. What's important is that you accept what's done is done and move on. There is nothing left. Although this card is often a sign that the worst is over, in some situations, the Ten of Swords is a fall from grace, backstabbing, or betrayal. It can also indicate being pinned down and unable to do anything about the current situation. For health readings, it's back trouble or surgery.

Reversed: Pick yourself up and start fresh. The situation has come to a close, and now you can recover. The Ten of Swords reversed promises a rebirth. Those swords have fallen out, and nothing is holding you back from a new life. The scars will heal in due time. But, of course, the other side of this reversal is refusing to seek care. You're fearful of what you might hear, so you ignore the problems. Or you play victim, crying "poor me" without accepting your role in your current circumstance.

Journaling prompt: What needs to come to a close at this time?

Page of Swords

The Page of Swords brings important news. Something is about to change, and you're getting the clarity you need. This is the precise diagnosis, the unvarnished truth, and the facts. The information will help you make confident decisions. This card can also mean the beginning of understanding or a new way of thinking. It's also intellectual curiosity: you might be interested in returning to school. Mental agility allows you to cut through the fog and get to the heart of a situation. Sharpen your focus and gather your tools for the job about to be done. This card can represent a mentally sharp individual or an alert pupil. In a reading about health, it suggests a minor surgery.

Reversed: Arguments break out over petty issues. Or you bend the truth because you don't want a conflict. Either way, the problems are minor and cannot be resolved if you don't confront the situation. In some cases, it might be time to cut ties. The Page of Swords reversed can also mean mental fogginess. You can't see clearly, or maybe you don't trust the information you're getting. It's possible you need a second opinion. I've also seen this card symbolize immaturity and intellectual snobbery.

Journaling prompt: What is the real story?

Knight of Swords

A hasty approach yields poor results. Sure, you want a quick answer, but if you push matters, you'll end up like the proverbial bull in a china shop. Temper your aggression and try not to act out until you have the facts. The Knight of Swords rushes into battle with his weapon drawn. This is a reasonable stance if you're fighting the good fight. But it's unlikely your point will be respected if you're trying to force your ideas on others. Be sure to evaluate your motives before diving into a conflict. This card can indicate important communication; sometimes, it could be bad news. Lastly, this Knight can suggest a situation that requires an aggressive approach. A solution can be found if you go in all the way.

Reversed: This reversal means you're fighting a losing battle. Why are you still in this? It may be time to give up and step away from the conflict. You're tired, or maybe the situation has gotten out of control. Chaos reigns, and you're losing your cool. You can no longer defend your position. Slow down, assess the current climate, and seek alternate routes. The Knight of Swords reversed can also represent a blowhard who loves to engage in straw man arguments or a rude sort who wants to dominate a situation. In some cases, this card can mean an accident caused by carelessness.

Journaling prompt: What am I fighting for?

QUEEN OF SWORDS.

Queen of Swords

The Queen of Swords knows how to speak out. This card says you can speak up for yourself and others. You can be a powerful advocate. Say what's on your mind. Ask all the right questions. Share your thoughts and do not hesitate to state what you feel about a situation or person. People are bound to listen to you. This card can represent a professional, someone with wisdom and experience. They will be a clear communicator, although sometimes a bit on the harsh side. You may not like what they say, but you will know where you stand. It can also represent a surgeon or mental health practitioner.

Reversed: Someone in your circle cannot be trusted. This is the card of the backstabber or the phony who doesn't have your best interests at heart. They are telling you what you want to hear or bending the truth to fulfill their own agenda. Perhaps they are only interested in what's in it for them, or maybe they lack empathy. Either way, you'll want to stay on high alert if you want to avoid trouble. Of course, you could hurt someone if you're the one playing this game. In older books, this was the card of the widow. This means the Queen of Swords reversed is associated with loss and grief, although they often suffer in silence.

Journaling prompt: What needs to be said?

King of Swords

KING OF SWORDS.

You can find a logical approach at this time. The King of Swords says: you see the writing on the wall, which allows for intelligent decision-making. The facts are laid bare, everything is clear, and you can proceed confidently. Make sure your head rules the heart as much as possible. Sometimes this card represents an experienced and wise person who cuts through the bull. They are the no-nonsense type and concerned with only what's real. This person might be a surgeon, doctor, lawyer, or other professional. Sometimes this card could indicate signing contracts or dealing with legal issues. In that case, you will need to be an advocate for yourself or others.

Reversed: The King of Swords could be someone who lacks sympathy or is just starting to get in touch with their feelings. They might seem cold, but, in time, you might discover they are holding back out of fear. They might be struggling to express their grief fully. Or they are fearful of being seen as weak, so they strike out and push others away. This reversal could also warn about the heart getting in the way or mental laziness. Sometimes, it can mean overturning legal decisions or problems with a settlement.

Journaling prompt: What is my head telling me in this situation?

Practice: In addition to the Death and Devil cards, no one likes to see the Swords suit pop up in a reading. These cards often fill people with fear. A great exercise to break down those assumptions is what I call "Good Card, Bad Card." Here's how it works: go through each card in the deck and find a positive and negative interpretation for the card. For example, the Sun could mean abundance or immaturity. The Ten of Swords can mean an ending or relief. I have found this practice to be helpful because it helps to avoid black-and-white thinking about the cards.

👁 **Pro tip:** Although you never want a querent to walk away from the Tarot table filled with anxiety, you also want to avoid pooh-poohing someone's fears about certain cards. For example, if someone expresses worry after seeing the Five of Swords, don't brush that concern aside with some pat statement about love and light. This is called *spiritual bypassing*, a practice that can cause harm. Instead, allow the querent to talk about why that card scares them. Then, I recommend they pick a card for advice. Often, this little bit of conversation and a new card can help the querent work through their fear in a healthy, proactive way.

ACE OF PENTACLES.

Ace of Pentacles

The Ace of Pentacles is traditionally viewed as a new source of income. But it can also be seen as a "helping hand." An offer is extended, which could move your life in a better direction. This card can also mean taking the first steps on a new path that has the potential for growth. You're planting seeds for your future. The Ace of Pentacles marks a favorable time for manifestation work or beginning anything worthwhile. Set new goals, take a different route, and commit to the life you want. The lush garden in this card is symbolic of fertility and abundance. Everything is possible. The Universe is handing you a gift.

Reversed: The Ace of Pentacles reversed is akin to a hand pulling away and closing into a tight fist. An offer is rescinded. The help is unavailable, or you may be fearful about asking for what you need. Instead of abundance, the resources are scarce. This could be putting you at a disadvantage. Another way of looking at this reversal is a false sense of security. You assume you're in a good position, but it's not as safe as you think. It's also possible you might be forced to weed out some aspects of your life if you wish to get to the root of a problem. Or maybe you're staying in the garden, dependent on others rather than trying to make your own way in the world. In that case, you'll want to think about ways you can find your footing again.

Journaling prompt: What opportunities can I say yes to right now?

Two of Pentacles

The figure in the Two of Pentacles juggles two coins while ships sail in the background on a turbulent ocean. This means you're in the midst of a busy, unpredictable time. You must remain adaptable because things could change at any moment. If you're trying to multitask or do it all, you might pull it off with a bit of fancy footwork. Take things as they come and remain nimble. It's also possible you are recalibrating after a significant change. Life will settle down as soon as you regain your sense of balance. For finances, the Two of Pentacles suggests difficult decisions ahead. Weigh every option carefully and be ready to shift things around as needed. If you have travel on your mind, this card can represent preparing for the journey.

Reversed: When you flip this card, the balance is lost. Finances are unstable, or you cannot stick to the current budget. Costs accelerate, leading to stress. This might be the right time to ask for help or to explore other options. If you cannot handle your responsibilities, is there someone who can step in? The Two of Pentacles reversed can also mean ignoring a financial situation or refusing to consider alternatives. You may also drop the ball and hope someone else cleans up the mess.

Journaling prompt: How can I create more ease?

Three of Pentacles

The Three of Pentacles is the classic card of collaboration. As the saying goes: teamwork makes the dream work. You have the right people at your side, and everyone works well together. As a result, everyone has an opportunity to shine brightly at this time. This doesn't necessarily have to do with a job. It can mean a health-care team or a family coming together for a specific goal. Whatever the case, you can be sure things will get done right. Sometimes the Three of Pentacles indicates developing new plans or projects. It can also mean taking pride in a job well done. In a spiritual reading, this card suggests the building of an inner temple or attending a service.

Reversed: The spirit of cooperation is lost. No one wants to work together, or the leadership is poor. Instead of focusing on shared goals, time is wasted squabbling over details. It's also possible the plans are unrealistic, or someone is actively sabotaging the situation. Nothing can happen until everyone can agree. This reversal can indicate a lack of goals or a botched job. Sometimes it can mean neglecting your duties or refusing to listen to sound advice.

Journaling prompt: How can I work better with others to get results that benefit all?

Four of Pentacles

Fours signify stability, and the Four of Pentacles shows fiscal security. You have what you need and feel in control at this time. Stability returns after a period of turmoil, and now you can build for the future. All of the resources you need to cover your bases are present. You're able to save for a rainy day and accumulate wealth. However, the shadow side of this card is the scarcity mindset, which may lead to hoarding. In that case, greed takes over, and you're unwilling to share what you have. Sometimes the Four of Pentacles means you need to protect your boundaries. If you feel threatened, shields up!

Reversed: When this reversal occurs, you must be ready and willing to let go. That could mean sharing your resources or relinquishing your need for control. It can also mean letting your guard down and allowing others in. The Four of Pentacles reversed can indicate that financial loss or expenses are more significant than initially thought. A new budget or loan may be necessary. I've also seen this card mean an estate sale or the distribution of assets. It can also represent a recluse or someone in quarantine. In a negative reading, it's the miser who refuses to help others.

Journaling prompt: What makes me feel safe?

Five of Pentacles

The Five of Pentacles is a card most folks don't like to get. It shows two people dressed in rags struggling to walk past a church in a snowstorm. One of the figures is on crutches. It's often a sign of financial loss or hardship. The resources you need are not available, which may cause stress. Or maybe you're coming out of a difficult period and need some help to get back on your feet. The good news: there is assistance right around the corner. Soon, things will change for the better. This card can also symbolize someone who sticks with you through the hard times. But the shadow side is being shut out. You've been kicked to the curb. You don't feel secure or included any longer. Another possible interpretation is injury or accidents. This card is always problematic, but hope is also present. You just need to look for it.

Reversed: When the Five of Pentacles is reversed, it indicates your situation changes for the better. You're coming in from the cold. Help is offered, and now you can start to rebuild your life. It can also mean a relationship goes through a change or the end of codependency. Just know whatever is happening now is for the best. For some, this card represents a time when you need to return to a hospital or rehab. Or maybe you're questioning your spiritual beliefs . . . or rejecting them.

Journaling prompt: What do I need to feel less anxious?

Six of Pentacles

The Six of Pentacles shows a change has happened to the unhoused people in the Five of Pentacles. Suddenly, a person of means is giving them money. This is the card of charity, sharing, and generosity. It's the benefactor coming through or the helping hand when you need it most. You may not be on your feet yet, but soon you will be. Or perhaps you're the one giving aid. In that case, you are in a position where you can give freely. The scales in the card symbolize justice—as in settling debts or legal affairs. But, of course, this can also represent social justice and the redistribution of wealth. The Six of Pentacles is an uneven power dynamic in a negative reading. One person controls others by keeping them dependent.

Reversed: This reversal shows a lack of help available. Finances are strained, and debts accumulate. Or a legal case falls apart, leading to loss. If you're getting sued or considering suing someone else, this is not the card you want to see. I've also seen this card mean an unfair inheritance, probate problems, or a contested will. In some cases, the Six of Pentacles reversed indicates poor financial management, such as giving to the point where it hurts you. In relationship readings, this shows roles being reversed, as in the caregiver needing care.

Journaling prompt: How can I share what I have in a balanced way?

Seven of Pentacles

A daunting period of work is ahead. You may need to take a step back to examine what needs to be done. Are things working? Or are you working hard for little gain? It may be time to rethink your plan. The Seven of Pentacles can also mean you're concerned about your financial situation. If that is the case, you might need to explore new ways to transform your current circumstances. This may require a new job or another source of income. The other side of this card is patience. Growth is on the way, but it's slow. In time, everything will blossom . . . as long as you keep up your reasonable efforts.

Reversed: When this reversal appears, you struggle to move past your work. There is no rest, which could lead to burnout. If you're overdoing it, now might be the time to enlist help. In some cases, this card means you feel lazy or uninspired. So you do the bare minimum and hope for results. When they don't come, you wonder what went wrong without looking at your role. For some, this is the card of the workaholic. Work becomes your god, and other things are neglected. Lastly, it can indicate worry or impatience.

Journaling prompt: Where do I need to work harder, and where can I ease up?

Eight of Pentacles

The Eight of Pentacles says you're working hard but don't mind. The reason why: You are seeing results. More importantly, you're doing what you love or doing work that you find interesting. Each day, your skills continue to grow. This marks a period of happy progress and excellence. If you have a to-do list, you will get through it little by little. The key is to have a plan and remain focused until each task is completed. This is the artisan, the person who is dedicated to their craft. In some readings, it can also mean hammering out a deal, as in negotiating a contract. It can also symbolize a skilled practitioner, who is able to do their work well.

Reversed: Instead of caring about your work, you rush through each project, unconcerned with quality. You may get everything done, but the quality will be shoddy. Mistakes are likely to be made if you insist on hastiness. Sometimes this reversal means a lack of work or losing your job due to poor performance. It can also symbolize an unskilled person who cannot provide your needed service. It's also possible finances could be holding up a situation. For example, the family may be unable to agree on an estate. Lastly, this card can also advise getting your affairs in order.

Journaling prompt: What skill do I want to develop?

Nine of Pentacles

The gorgeous Nine of Pentacles shows the good life. You are victorious and able to enjoy the fruits of your hard labor. Or perhaps you receive a windfall, which creates ease. Now you can relax. This could be a period of rest or time spent alone. You're comfortable in every sense of the word and have everything you need or want. For some, this card can mean retirement. Whatever your situation, you are settled and secure. Be grateful.

Reversed: You have what you need, so you don't feel interested in growing it further. Maybe you're lazy. Or perhaps you are taking your situation for granted. For some, this reversal means your goals do not come to fruition, whereas others may feel the grass is greener on the other side. The Nine of Pentacles reversed can mean a loss of position or a financial situation with strings attached. For example, you have a benefactor, and they control your every move. This card can also represent vultures hanging around a loved one, hoping to receive an inheritance.

Journaling prompt: How can I enjoy myself more?

Ten of Pentacles

The Ten of Pentacles shows a scene with a family in a lovely garden setting. This means the family is united. Everyone is secure and safe. The elders are cared for as well as the children. Perhaps you're living in a communal situation. A family reunion is possible. There may be a reason to come together in a spirit of celebration. Of course, this card can mean financial abundance. A legacy passed down through generations. Another way of looking at the Ten of Pentacles is the journey's end. You fulfilled your destiny. Now you can rest.

Reversed: In this card, security means nothing. You walk away from it or choose to abandon the family. Maybe the situation is too toxic. Or perhaps you're the outsider and have been written out of the will. This can also mean neglect. You're not taking care of your home or the family. Instead, you're doing your own thing. Sometimes this reversal means a family feud. The stability is lost, and the conflicts remain. An unhealthy dynamic where no one feels cared for or safe.

Journaling prompt: What does family mean to me?

PAGE OF PENTACLES.

Page of Pentacles

The Page of Pentacles is an excellent card to see if you are learning a new skill. The Page of Pentacles is the apt pupil who can absorb information and gather more experience. You might be embarking on a new endeavor, or maybe you're planting new seeds for the future. Risks might need to be taken, but you have solid ground beneath your feet. This is a time to develop new plans. Sometimes this card symbolizes a bright young person with a studious mind. Because Pages are messengers, another interpretation is good news, especially concerning financial situations.

Reversed: Your head is not in the game. You've lost concentration and cannot seem to focus. This lack of focus could lead to mistakes. Perhaps you're bored, or maybe you're burned out. Either way, you need to ground yourself if you want to avoid trouble. The Page of Pentacles reversed can mean receiving news you don't like. It can also indicate being too dependent on others. In this case, you cannot care for yourself or might be taking other people for granted. Unrealistic goals and a lack of preparation for the future are different ways to view this card.

Journaling prompt: What can I learn from this current circumstance?

KNIGHT OF PENTACLES.

Knight of Pentacles

Of all the Knights, the Knight of Pentacles is the only one who is not in motion. That doesn't mean things are not happening. Instead, the progress is slow and steady. There is a rooted energy present, which allows for solid decision-making. You know what needs to be done and take all the right actions. This is not a time for risk. Instead, a pragmatic approach is best. The Knight of Pentacles can symbolize a reliable person who offers support, perhaps financial. They are a solid rock when you need them the most. Lastly, this card symbolizes a time when you are "in your body" and fully present.

Reversed: Instead of progress, you're stuck in the mud and unwilling to budge. You might be choosing to remain in a situation that doesn't benefit you. Or perhaps you want to be correct, so you'll stay put to prove a point. The Knight of Pentacles reversed can mean bickering over money or draining your resources on foolish things. This card sometimes signals an impractical attitude, such as indulging in "get rich quick" schemes instead of doing the work. This Knight can also symbolize a loafer or person always looking for something new instead of appreciating what they have right now.

Journaling prompt: How can I create more stability?

Queen of Pentacles

QUEEN OF PENTACLES.

This Queen says: you're secure. Not much bothers you at this time. You're taking care of what matters and not concerned with petty stuff. You're too busy securing your kingdom for that. You may be conserving both energy and resources. Under your watchful eye, the hearth and home remain safe and prosperous. The Queen of Pentacles can symbolize a dutiful caregiver, loving parent, or trustworthy professional. It's someone you can count on. In the image, you can see many plants blooming, a sign of success and fertility. Every seed you planted is growing. Keep tending to your goals, and you'll continue to turn a profit.

Reversed: Instead of the meticulous and practical nature of the upright version, this card means poor habits, laziness, and a slovenly approach. You're not taking care of yourself or your environment. You let it all go to hell. This is the caregiver who doesn't do their job or the neglectful parent. On the flip side, this reversal can symbolize a helicopter parent or control freak who micromanages every detail to the point where nothing gets done. Nothing is ever good enough! The Queen of Pentacles reversed can indicate financial dependence on others or an inability to prepare for the future.

Journaling prompt: What needs attention right now?

KING OF PENTACLES.

King of Pentacles

You've mastered a financial situation. Now you have the resources you need to feel secure. Everything is growing underneath your feet, enabling you to provide well. This is the card of the responsible and talented leader or the trustworthy professional. They are sturdy, grounded, and an authority in their field. If you are focusing on building wealth, it's a great card. It means you can attain all of your material goals. You have sound judgement and integrity. All of the growth you're experiencing is due to your thoughtful planning and hard work. Enjoy what you have. You've earned it!

Reversed: Instead of security, this King is a miser, or they lack the funds altogether. This can mean financial mismanagement, gambling, or problems caused by other people's foolish decisions. Now you are left to clean up the mess left behind. Sometimes this King uses money as a weapon, or they may use wealth in a corrupt way. This card symbolizes a scarcity mentality or interest in controlling others via money. The King of Pentacles reversed is the greedy person who engages in shady behavior. Think of it as a Bernie Madoff type who profits while harming others.

Journaling prompt: How can I manage my resources to create security for myself and those I love?

Practice: Pentacles are excellent for affirmation work. Here's what to do: go through each card in the Pentacles suit and create a positive affirmation centered on security or abundance. For example, the Eight of Pentacles might be "I have a stable, fulfilling career." The Five of Pentacles could be "I have enough money to help others in need." Write down your affirmations and paste them in a place where you can see them. If you'd like, keep the card out as a reminder of the energy you're trying to conjure. (Psst, you can do this with any of the cards in the deck!)

Pro tip: Sometimes querents can become dependent on the cards. You need to discourage this behavior. That means you must keep professional boundaries tight. For example, you might need to limit how often someone can come and see you. Don't feel bad about setting limits. Healthy boundaries will ensure folks are living their lives rather than relying on Tarot to live it for them.

PART TWO

SPREADS FOR GUIDANCE

HOW TO DEAL WHEN
LIFE GETS REAL

A S I MENTIONED IN MY INTRODUCTION, this is a book about hope. It is about how Tarot can give you the support you need so you can live well when life seems to be handing you all the hard cards. Because ultimately, that's the bottom line: when you are *really* living, you are present. Only then can you care deeply for others and be at peace with your own mortality. That is really living.

This section pulls back the curtain on the stuff professional tarot readers regularly deal with—in other words real life. Yes, people will always want predictive readings (job? marriage? purchases?), but in the realm of counseling and guidance, this book will share what I've learned from decades of working with clients. It will share best practices and insights. It will also guide you through some "dos" and "don'ts."

The majority of spreads discussed in this section are simple 3- to 5-card spreads, which are read from left to right.

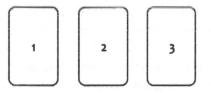

Where the layout is more specialized, I've provide diagrams for the spread.

Daily Pulls and Journaling

Before we dive into each topic, I want to discuss the wisdom of the *daily pull* (aka *daily draw*; I use the terms interchangeably). Pulling a daily card is an excellent way to center yourself and create an intentional day. It's also a fantastic method for learning to read Tarot or for seasoned pros to keep their reading chops strong.

I prefer to do this first thing in the morning, but you may like the afternoon or evening instead. Starting your day with a pull sets the tone for a mindful approach to your day, while an evening pull might help reflect on the day's events. Either way is acceptable.

The daily draw doesn't require a lot of effort. All you need is your favorite deck, a journal, and a pen.

Here's the process: Begin centering yourself by taking three deep breaths. Inhale through the nose and exhale through the mouth slowly. Feel yourself settling into your body.

Shuffle the cards in a way that feels natural for you. I like to keep my eyes closed to tune in to my energy. When you are ready, stop shuffling. Put the deck facedown. Using your left hand, cut the deck into three piles. Then restack them any way you like.

Choose the card from the top of the deck. Turn it over, and without stopping to overthink, begin journaling anything that comes to mind. For example, if you pull the Page of Pentacles, maybe you're thinking about a young person in your life, or you have a money situation on your mind. Don't overanalyze; just free write.

Describe what's happening on the card, list the symbols that catch your eye, and write about how you feel that morning or how the image on the card reflects your mood. Again: just write.

You can do this like Julia Cameron's *Morning Pages* and fill three pages with your thoughts. Or perhaps you want to write only a few lines. There are no rules.

When you feel done, close your journal, put down your pen, and leave the card where you can see it throughout your day. You may tuck it away and carry it with you. That's fine too.

As you go about your day, look for how the card might appear. For example, if you wrote about a young person using the model here, notice your interactions with any children you encounter. Pay attention.

At the end of the day, revisit your notes. How did Tarot show up in your world? Did the practice help you remain present and intentional? If not, why? Do you feel your interpretations were accurate, or can you find new meanings based on your experiences?

I highly recommend getting into this practice. Doing so will strengthen your relationship with the Tarot and with your inner wisdom. After all, Tarot is simply a tool to help you get there.

Practice: Try doing a daily pull for a week. Notice if there is a certain Tarot theme popping up throughout the week. For example, are you getting mostly Cups? If so, how did that play out? At the end of the week, tally up the cards and look for patterns or cycles. You might be surprised!

TAROT FOR ILLNESS
AND HEALING

When the unthinkable happens, the lighthouse is hope.
Once we choose hope, everything is possible.

—CHRISTOPHER REEVE

A FEW YEARS AGO, I was on a trip with my husband. We were in Portland for a confer-
ence, and when we weren't at the event, much of our time was spent exploring the
city. One of our favorite activities is walking around randomly and discovering nooks,
crannies, and cute neighborhoods. We also like to stumble into interesting, out-of-the-
way restaurants. On this particular day, my goal was to find something I'd never tried
before. Plus, my stomach was rumbling.

Instead of our usual clipped pace, my husband moved along like a tired old slug.
I began to get irritated as he fell behind again and again. It didn't help that he didn't
explain what was going on. Instead, he simply said, "I need to catch my breath."

Finally, he said he wasn't feeling well and wanted to rest at the hotel. It was appar-
ent he wasn't his usual self, so we cut our adventure short so that he could give his body
time to recalibrate. After a nap, I assumed he'd be up and at 'em, but the same problem
persisted the rest of the trip. The busy airport was a nightmare, so I was grateful I scheduled plenty of layover time to get to each terminal. We needed it.

When we got home, he seemed to be okay. But then again, we were not hoofing
around cities and airports, so it was easy to miss the signs. The only hint I got that something was really wrong was when he used the stairs. He would be breathless in short
order, which was troubling because he appeared physically fit. When I expressed concern, he waved it off. Until one day, it got scary, he admitted it had become a chronic
problem, and he was nervous.

We made an appointment immediately, and he received a diagnosis and treatment. Unfortunately, his condition is serious and chronic, but the new medication has made it tolerable.

I cannot imagine what would have happened if he hadn't told me how he felt. He's the stoic type, so he didn't want to worry me. Plus, ignoring the problem was his preferred method of dealing with anxiety. Our life has changed dramatically since then, but we are dealing with our new circumstances with practicality and plenty of love.

When you get a scary diagnosis from the doctor, it can flip your life inside out. Or, equally distressing is the time when something is clearly wrong, but doctors are stumped, and nobody can give you a clear diagnosis. That's just as hard, if not worse. Illness can leave us feeling stunned, wondering, "Why me?" and "What now?"

Other emotions such as anger, denial, and depression are common too. It's important to deal with these feelings, first and foremost, whether you are recently diagnosed or dealing with an ongoing situation or treatment.

You may be tempted to hold in your feelings, but often this makes the situation worse. Plus, it doesn't allow folks to support you. Learning how to accept help and adapt to your situation is never easy.

I learned this lesson myself when I sprained my foot earlier this year. My typical method of operation is rushing around with too many things in my arms. I consider this "efficient," but my mother always said it was dangerous. That day, I was holding a bunch of boxes, which obscured my vision as I began descending the stairs in the back hall.

My foot missed a step, and suddenly, I found myself flat on my back with my foot twisted and starting to swell. I screamed for my husband, and he helped me get back up the stairs to assess the damage. It was significant. Although the foot wasn't broken, it was soon black and blue and twice its size.

Needless to say, this swollen foot threw a major wrench in the operation of our household. I could no longer do all the things. Instead, I was on a walker for weeks as I attempted to scoot around in a house that was nothing but stairs. Like my husband, I tend to be cool-headed regarding these sorts of things. But I knew this wasn't going to be wise. Especially since he couldn't exactly run around for me. I had to rely on my children to lift the load until I healed. That meant I needed to ask for help.

I also relied on my friends for emotional support, which kept my spirits up while I regained my ability to walk all over again. Self-care was the only thing I really *could* do at this time. Of course, Tarot played a considerable role in my healing—much as it did when I played the caregiver role for my loved ones. My daily readings were a spiritual check-in while my body tried to mend itself. It took time, but eventually, I could get back on my feet and strengthen my ankle.

Tarot was my ally, reminding me of when I needed to put myself first, ask for support, or slow down. Every day, I pulled a personal card and followed the wisdom. My healing was gradual, but Tarot kept me centered. The recovery period became deeply spiritual as I began to look within at all the emotions I was feeling about my situation . . . and my husband's. I came to terms with fear, sadness, and the prospect of getting older and frailer. These are not easy things to face, but illness or injury requires introspection. After all, you're healing more than the body.

This journey has been humbling, but Tarot has given me perspective. While it's never a substitute for medical care, it can be self-care, an essential tool for wellness.

How to Give an Effective Reading Around Health and Healing

Tarot can be helpful when you or someone you love is unwell. But it must be used wisely. That begins with recognizing Tarot is not meant to diagnose an illness or prescribe treatment. While the cards can sometimes see a problem, the reading is never a guarantee, especially since humans are notorious for misinterpretation. The only way to get an accurate diagnosis is by visiting your health-care practitioner. (Psst, they'll sometimes admit that science doesn't know everything either!)

Trying to get a diagnosis through Tarot is no better than searching those internet health sites and looking for symptoms that match yours. I've been guilty of that myself! Every time I go that route, I end up down a medical rabbit hole, convinced I have a terminal disease. This is not what to do when you feel unwell. Sometimes you might be tempted to treat your Tarot deck like WebMD, but I can assure you, that approach will probably cause more fear than relief. A quick trip to a specialist will give you the answer.

An effective reading about health and illness always begins with knowing our limits as Tarot readers. That advice may sound simple, but it's true. When you remain humble in your approach, you are more likely to find or offer information that heals rather than harms.

Can You Predict Illness with Tarot?

I get this question a lot. However, while cards can portend illness, such as the Ten of Swords for back trouble, the Three of Swords for heart problems, or the Tower for an accident, most professional readers shy away from them due to ethical concerns. There is always the chance you are wrong and may cause undue anxiety for the querent (or yourself). So I would probably say it's wise to step carefully around making predictions about health. If you sense a potential health problem, it's best to deliver what you see with a delicate touch.

For example, suppose the Three of Swords comes up in a reading. I might ask the client when they last had a checkup. This question can open up the door for a conversation. Without alarming them, I would say, "The cards indicate you need to get a checkup around your heart." Suppose the client has further questions or seems worried. In that case, I'll usually say: "I'm not a doctor, but this card tells me you need to pay more attention to your well-being so you can avoid trouble, and the best way to do that is by making an appointment with your health-care practitioner."

Many times, I've delivered information in this manner, and the querent saw the doctor and learned they needed surgery or some other treatment. These people were grateful that I pointed out the potential problem without scaring them. A practical and compassionate approach without doom and gloom can be just the nudge someone needs to make better decisions about their health.

Sometimes people ask about health because they are secretly worried about something. They hope Tarot will either show a good outcome or confirm their fears. Either case puts the Tarot reader in an uncomfortable position. Therefore, it's best to be up front with the querent and ask them what they are concerned about or hoping from the reading. This way, you better understand the motive behind the question.

In my experience, most folks who wanted readings about illness already knew they were unwell. They might have a chronic condition or perhaps a new diagnosis, and they were up front about the situation rather than playing a guessing game. These readings have a different feel than the ones where people want a prediction. In these cases, the querent is usually more pragmatic about their situation and is looking for support on their journey. These readings tend to be meaningful for both querent and the reader.

In short, it's best not to make a prediction but rather to look at the energy present in the reading. If the cards look stormy, encourage the querent to seek professional help. You never know . . . you might just save a life. That life could be your own too, if you're inquiring about your health.

Questions About Wellness

When asking questions about wellness, you'll want to keep these truths in mind: yes/no questions are rarely helpful. Same with "Will I?" These questions lead to black-and-white answers, and healing is rarely that simple. This is a fatalistic approach, which often leads to fear-based decisions. "Should I?" is also unhelpful because it puts the responsibility firmly in the reader's lap or the cards, when those decisions should be made only with a licensed professional.

For example, "Will I get well?" might seem like a good question, but what if you don't like the cards that show up? Will that cause you to panic or fall into a depression? How would you convey that info to a frightened client who might be secretly worried they will never recuperate? A better reframe would be, "What can I do to support my healing at this time?" This approach puts the power back in your hands or the hands of the querent. Keep in mind that folks often feel powerless when dealing with illness. This is why you want to look for ways to help remain present and empowered.

Here's another example of a question that doesn't belong on the Tarot table: "Should I stop taking my medication?" I've been asked this question on more than one occasion. But, unfortunately, this question puts you in a dangerous position as a Tarot reader if you say yes. For the querent, it's potentially putting their health in the hands of an unqualified person. So it's best to refrain from this line of questioning altogether, especially around treatment.

Here are some sample questions that open the door for meaningful conversations and helpful readings:

What is my body trying to tell me?

How can I take better care of myself at this time?

What is the greatest lesson that I can learn from this difficult ordeal?

What do I need to remember as I move along through this healing journey?

Notice there are no yes/no questions here. Also, none of the "Will I?" or "Should I?" types. Instead, these are some of my favorite questions for this topic.

Practice: Consider some questions you might ask Tarot if you're not well. What are some things you could ask? Also, take some time to consider what someone might ask you if they are facing a scary diagnosis. How could Tarot help in that situation?

What to Say and What Not to Say

A compelling Tarot reading also requires a bit of common sense and a gentle approach when it comes to delivering information about illness. For many folks, it's hard to know what to say when someone announces they are unwell. We often resort to platitudes, which show we mean well but leave the other person feeling dismissed.

It's essential to create an atmosphere of trust and support, and that begins with knowing what to say and what not to. So here are a few suggestions on what to say and what to avoid.

What to Say:

I'm sorry you are going through this. I'm here for you.

Let me know what you need and what you don't need.

I love you and hate that you're unwell.

What are some of the things I can do to make your life easier right now?

I really admire how you're handling this.

What Not to Say:

You might have manifested this through negative thinking. Throw some love and light at it!

Well, it could be worse.

Have you tried this all-natural treatment?

You look great; you don't look sick to me!

Wow, you look awful.

Everything is going to be fine!

My mother had the same problem, and she had a total recovery!

Also, sometimes it's best to simply listen. Give them space to talk, vent, or name their emotions. Be utterly present without thinking about how you will react or what to say. Presence is a gift, and for someone who is struggling with their health, your presence can be good medicine.

Talking about your feelings may be hard if you are dealing with a health issue. You might also feel uneasy asking for help. Please know your loved ones might not know how to assist you or what to say. You may need to open the door for uncomfortable conversations if they won't or can't. It sucks when you have to do that, but playing the stoic card won't help you . . . or them.

Instead, treat these conversations as part of your healing practice. By naming your feelings and needs, you are creating the conditions for meaningful connections, which can make all the difference as you navigate this tender time.

Journaling prompt: What are some ways you can better support someone who is dealing with an illness? If you're dealing with a health crisis, what might be some things you need right now, and how can you ask for help?

Practice: If a loved one is currently dealing with poor health, take some time to anticipate their needs rather than asking them to tell you what they need. When you have an idea of how you can best help, simply say: "I have Tuesday free. Let me come over, clean the house, run your errands, and cook dinner." This approach will offer support without putting the burden of asking on your loved one, who probably has a lot on their mind.

Pro tip: Not all illnesses are visible. Just because someone "looks well" doesn't mean they are. When folks sit down at your Tarot table, assumptions about what an "unwell person" looks like should be avoided.

Now let's explore a few helpful spreads.

Daily Pull

As I stated earlier, a daily card reading can help guide your day. More importantly, it centers you in the present, which is crucial when dealing with health issues. I also highly recommend the Body Mind Spirit spread for regular check-ins.

Body Mind Spirit Spread

The Body Mind Spirit is a well-known spread that works well for assessing your overall energy. It gives a glimpse into your physical, mental, and spiritual state, and that information can guide you into making excellent decisions.

I use the Body Mind Spirit spread all the time, both when I'm feeling well . . . or not. It's also one of the first spreads I turn to when moving through a challenging round of responsibilities. Taking a moment to check my well-being is a form of self-care. Use this Tarot layout any time you need to see where you are and what you need.

Here's what to do: Shuffle the cards in a way that feels natural and relaxed. If this is difficult, you can have a caregiver shuffle for you. Breathe deeply and quiet your mind. When you feel ready, stop shuffling and put the deck facedown in front of you.

Using your left hand, cut the deck into three piles. If that's not possible, you can use the other hand or ask your caregiver to cut the deck.

Put the cards back into one pile, any way you wish. Then fan the deck out, still facedown.

Run your hands over the cards and let your intuition pick one for each position: Body, Mind, and Spirit. Turn the cards over and take a moment to study the images. What stands out? Which card catches your eye? How are the three cards interacting . . . or not? What story is unfolding? Consider these prompts for a minute or as long as you need.

Then interpret the cards.

What if you get "bad" cards? Good question! I like to say there is no such thing as a bad card, but some of the images can be frightening. In those cases, choose three more as "advice" for the other cards.

Here's a sample reading: Leon has been struggling with a chronic illness for a few years. Often, it leaves him drained and unable to perform basic tasks. He has medication, which helps, but he still has days when he's too exhausted to function. Here are the cards he drew on a tough day.

Body: Seven of Cups reversed—Sevens symbolize a challenge, and the Pentacles suit is associated with the earth element. Reversed, the vibe becomes ungrounded. This means he may feel "out of his body," something Leon says he struggles with on days when he has taken on too much work. However, sometimes he continues to push himself even though his body says to stop and rest. He's been doing that lately, and this card shows he could experience an energy crash if he keeps ignoring the signals his body sends him.

Mind: Page of Pentacles—Interestingly, Leon is grounded when it comes to his mind. The Page of Pentacles is firmly planted on the earth and concentrates intensely on the coin in their hands. This shows mental focus and practicality. It also means Leon's mind remains alert, even when his body is giving out. Leon admits he can get wrapped up in a task, which will cause him to ignore how his body feels.

Spirit: Two of Swords reversed—Sitting quietly might be helpful at this time, but that's not something he is doing at the moment. A busy life means spiritual practices are probably neglected, which adds to the ungrounded feeling. Leon says he has been juggling work and school, so other things in his life have taken a back seat. For him to be balanced, he needs to devote more time to just being instead of constantly doing.

The cards are clearly showing a person who is heading toward burnout.

Leon wasn't too fond of these cards, even though the Page of Pentacles is rock solid. So he decided to choose three more cards as advice. But, again, choosing more cards isn't necessary unless you feel you need additional guidance.

Body: King of Cups—When you combine this card with the Seven of Cups reversed, it says: pay attention at all times to how you feel. Your emotions are the key to keeping your body functioning well. There may still be ups and downs with your energy, but you can figure out how to go with the flow wisely if you remain alert to ebbs and flows.

Mind: King of Pentacles—This is a fabulous card combined with the Page of Pentacles. Leon seems to be in a good place mentally. Perhaps his studies and the stimulating nature of his work keep him healthily engaged with the world.

Spirit: Three of Cups—Getting back into the community could help support Leon spiritually. It's been a minute since he's visited the Buddhist temple he used to belong to. Perhaps it's time to go back and gain the support that his spirit needs. Also, social activity with his fellow meditators might remind him there is more to life than work.

This information is giving Leon the cue that something needs to change now. The sooner he slows down, the better he will feel.

Practice: Try out this Body Mind Spirit spread and journal your thoughts. If you like, you can keep the cards out and revisit them at the end of the day. Did you heed their advice? If so, how did that change your experience? If not, what did you learn?

Pro tip: If you use this spread with a client, rather than trying to predict how they are feeling, allow them to talk about what the card reveals about their situation. For example, say you pull the Ace of Pentacles reversed for the Mind position. Instead of interpreting it, ask, "What do you feel this says about your state of mind at this time?" This question allows the querent a chance to both reflect and discuss what's going on. It also helps you maintain good ethics and boundaries.

The Chakra Spread

If you've studied yoga, you're probably familiar with the chakras. *Chakra* is a Sanskrit word that means wheel or cycle. They are "energy centers" in the astral body, located along the spine, from the tailbone to the crown of the head.

You cannot see or touch the chakras because they are not physical. There are seven main chakras in the body, and each one corresponds to a color as well as the physical, psychological, and spiritual parts of our lives. When the chakras are "spinning" correctly, we are in harmony with that part of our life. But when they are "blocked," or not moving in the right direction, we might feel off and need to invest in self-care or consult a health-care practitioner. The Chakra spread is the one I use to see if there is an imbalance. I find it can give clear answers to possible physical, emotional, or spiritual issues. Keep in mind that it is not for diagnosing or prescribing. Instead, we're exploring how the energy is flowing.

Like the Body Mind Spirit spread, this one is excellent for checking in with yourself.

Following our previous instructions, you'll want to take your time shuffling the cards. When you feel ready, put the deck facedown on the table in front of you. Cut the deck into three piles and put them back together any way you like. Then take seven cards from the top of the deck and put them in a vertical row, starting with the first one on the bottom.

Here are the positions:

Card 1: Root Chakra. Red. Your basic needs, survival, and identity.

Card 2: Sacral Chakra. Orange. Creativity, pleasure, and desire.

Card 3: Solar Plexus Chakra. Yellow. Willpower, self-esteem, and autonomy.

Card 4: Heart Chakra. Green. Love, compassion, and the ability to connect with others.

Card 5: Throat Chakra. Blue. Communication, self-expression, and truth.

Card 6: Third Eye Chakra. Indigo. Intuition, imagination, and the ability to see the big picture.

Card 7: Crown Chakra. Purple. Awareness, knowledge, and wisdom.

Here's a sample: Nia is recovering from a minor accident. She hurt her shoulder but, thankfully, didn't need surgery. Instead, she had to take it easy and wear a brace. She is rested up after a few weeks off from work, but she wants to check in with her energy before heading back to the office.

Here is her reading:

Card 1: Root Chakra. Seven of Pentacles—This healing journey has been challenging, especially because Nia loves her job. Also, being on unemployment meant she had less income during this time. The Seven of Pentacles indicates there is concern about her security. However, she knows getting back to work will change her money situation.

Card 2: Sacral Chakra. Knight of Swords reversed—The need to sit still and care for herself was more complicated than she thought. This card shows mental challenges around rest, recovery, and self-care. Nia admits she felt lazy during her convalescence. Her struggles to let go of the need to be doing made it hard for Nia to give herself as much self-love as she needed. This is something she'll need to work on as she heads back to the office.

Card 3: Solar Plexus Chakra. King of Pentacles—Nia derives her identity through her career and ability to provide for the household. This is where her self-worth is tied up. No wonder she has trouble with the second chakra! The King of Pentacles shows Nia's work has a grounding influence on her.

Card 4: Heart Chakra. Ten of Swords—It's interesting to see this card because the Heart Chakra is located on the sternum, right between the shoulders. To me, this card indicates Nia still has healing left to do here. She also confesses she felt cut off from people while she was recuperating. Getting out of the house and back to work will be great for her heart.

Card 5: Throat Chakra. King of Cups—Nia has no trouble expressing what's in her heart. She speaks her truth and leads with intention. She kept in touch with friends and coworkers while healing, so even though she missed folks, she wasn't lonely.

Card 6: Third Eye Chakra. Two of Swords—There might be a blockage here. After all, the figure in the Two of Swords has a blindfold over the eyes! The accident left Nia with a feeling of trepidation. She doesn't trust herself as much because she thinks the situation could have been avoided if she had only paid attention to her instincts.

Card 7: Crown Chakra. Knight of Pentacles—Despite the Two of Swords in the Third Eye position, this card indicates she's learned a valuable lesson from her experience. She's coming out of her healing period with practical wisdom she can apply going forward and a new appreciation for her job and the connections it provides for her.

Overall, Nia seems to be doing fine. But it's obvious: she's ready to get to work because that's where she feels valued.

Practice: There are many great resources on chakras. My absolute favorite is *Eastern Body, Western Mind: Psychology and the Chakra System as a Path to the Self* by Anodea Judith. The information in this book complements this reading beautifully. I highly recommend getting a copy.

Ritual . . . .

Pendulum Ritual. Pendulums are a fantastic way to check in with your chakras. I have used this method for myself and others, and it works. Here's what you do. You can sit in a chair if you're performing this ritual on yourself. For another person, they should lie flat on their back. Hold the pendulum firmly in your dominant hand with your thumb and index finger. Keep the pendulum still as you hover it above the first chakra, located at the pubic bone. Soon, the pendulum will begin to spin. The chakra is moving fine if it turns in a clockwise, even manner. If the pendulum spins counterclockwise, in a haphazard motion, or doesn't move, the energy center is blocked.

Do this for each chakra and note which ones need attention. There are two ways to get the energy moving properly for those chakras. First, you can gently lay your hands on the chakra while visualizing it turning around and moving clockwise. When you can "see" that, move on to the next. (If you are doing this ritual for someone else, please ask for permission before you touch them. If they don't want you to lay your hands on them, instruct them to do it themselves.) The other option is breathing deeply into the chakra, visualizing a flower's opening petals. Once you can see that in your mind's eye, continue to breathe deeply while picturing the flower beginning to spin clockwise. Repeat for each one. These methods have always worked for me. Of course, if you feel as if something is off, be sure to consult with your health-care practitioner.

Recovery Spread

You may feel scared when you are in recovery, whether from surgery, illness, or addiction. Afraid as in "What if this doesn't work?" or "What if it comes back again?" Rather than feeling healed, you're stressing out about an uncertain future. If you find yourself in that headspace, use this simple Recovery spread to untangle your thinking:

Card 1: Present moment

Card 2: What do I need right now?

Card 3: How can I continue to support my healing?

Rashid is completing his last round of chemotherapy. The doctor has given him a good prognosis, and he wants to continue moving in the right direction. But, of course, he is nervous about his situation. Here is his reading:

Card 1: Present moment. Ten of Cups—This is a positive card, one that shows he's moving toward complete healing. Rashid has the right support system and health-care team by his side. The optimistic prognosis is aligned with this card. It's time to celebrate!

Card 2: What do I need right now? Page of Swords reversed—Rashid admits he is a worrier by nature. This card indicates that when he gets in his head, dark clouds seem to form. So it's essential to stay alert for those times when he starts to spiral. If he can do that, he can remain focused on his healing and how well things are actually going.

Card 3: How can I continue to support my healing? Nine of Pentacles—Rashid is on the right path at this time. In fact, he seems to be flourishing. The most important thing is to continue until the treatment is complete and, in the meantime, stop and smell the roses. Staying in the present moment, which is good, will help him continue to thrive at this time.

Practice: The questions in this spread are excellent for journaling too. Be sure to keep your journal handy and free write whatever comes to mind as you reflect on the questions and the cards drawn.

Pro tip: When people are in recovery, they are vulnerable. You need to be extra mindful of the words you choose, especially if you sense fear. This doesn't mean reading the cards through rose-colored glasses. You can be honest without triggering folks.

The Waiting Room

As I mentioned before in the Hanged One, waiting rooms are anxious places. I know whenever I've been in one, the vibe is palpable. It's too easy to start imagining all the things that might happen if you're the one coming for treatment. It's equally challenging when you're playing the supporting role during a loved one's visit.

For me, the dental office is one of the hardest places to be. I have had significant issues in my mouth, which has required a tremendous amount of time spent in the dentist's chair. Sitting in the office always leaves me with a feeling of dread. Of course, my imagination always finds the darkest places to linger. However, I started to do a simple practice to help me stay centered and calm: I carry a mini Tarot card with me, usually the Star, a card of hope, healing, and optimism.

The next time you're going in, tuck a copy of the Star or any other card you like as a talisman. Knowing it's in my pocket keeps me centered and not going into worse case scenario thinking.

Other cards I like for this practice: the Sun, Six of Wands, Four of Wands, or the World.

Ritual . . . .

Anointing with Oil. When I was recovering from my foot injury, my friend Bradetta sent me a bottle of magical oil with arnica, St. John's wort, and lavender. Every day after my shower, I would sit and rub this oil on my feet, saying "I love you" and "thank you" repeatedly. The combination of the oil, massage, and words of affirmation helped my healing process.

Try this ritual when you're recuperating. You can use any oil you like. I find it's best to do this right after a hot shower or bath. Before bedtime works well too. Put a few drops of oil into the palm of your hand and then gently rub it into the body part that needs your attention. Repeat "I love you" and "thank you" while you continue massaging the oil into your skin. You can also start listing all the reasons why you're grateful for that body part, or you can use an affirmation such as "My foot is completely healed." Do this daily as long as you like.

If you cannot rub the oil on yourself, have a caregiver do it while you recite your positive affirmations. You can choose to state them silently to yourself.

Breathwork/Meditation

Sitting with sound. Illness can bring up many unpleasant feelings: fear, anxiety, and depression. You can be tempted to check out, but this is the time when you need to be present. Breathwork and meditation can help soothe frazzled nerves and keep you centered as you work on healing.

A practice that I like is what I call "sitting with sound." Begin by sitting or lying in a comfortable position. Take a few deep breaths through the nostrils and exhale slowly through your mouth. This will help to settle your energy.

Then begin to notice the sound around you. You might hear the whir of the air conditioner or a dog barking outside. Maybe you'll hear an obnoxious car horn if you live in a busy city. Try not to judge these sounds. Simply observe. Let these sounds come and go without trying to hold on. After a few minutes, open your eyes and notice how you feel.

Fun story: I was teaching a yoga class one day, and just as I began leading a meditation, we were treated to the rat-a-tat-tat of a jackhammer outside the studio window. Immediately, the students started to tense up and gripe. I instructed them to listen closely to the noise and use that as their meditation. As soon as they started to tune into the sound, they relaxed. It worked!

TAROT FOR CAREGIVING

There are only four kinds of people in the world.
Those who have been caregivers. Those who are currently caregivers.
Those who will be caregivers, and those who will need a caregiver.

—ROSALYN CARTER

W HEN SOMEONE GETS ILL, whether it's cancer or anything else, they typically receive an outpouring of support from loved ones—as they should.

But caregivers need support just as much as the unwell person. Unfortunately, caregivers are usually overlooked and depleted, often ending up sick. The reason is that they can be reluctant to ask for help. (I speak from experience!)

According to a National Library of Medicine study in 2018–2019, more than 31 percent of registered nurses report extreme burnout, with symptoms including insomnia, sadness, anger, fatigue, and (often) self-medicating and substance abuse. Plenty of people who aren't nurses—moms, dads, parents, and adult children—experience this kind of burnout too. This is what happens to people who care deeply and give all they can . . . unless they take precautions to protect themselves.

As I alluded to, I know this story all too well. My mother was a sickly woman with a childhood filled with a never ending series of hospital visits. In addition to heart trouble, she had epilepsy, with severe seizures that left her too weak to go to school.

When I was young, all hell broke loose as she needed open heart surgery to repair a leaky valve in her heart. I remember being shuttled off to my aunt's farm with my siblings while Dad waited at the hospital for news. She pulled through that operation, but a few years later, she needed another one. I don't recall the details of that procedure. Still, I remember her staggering to the phone to call the ambulance a few days later when her stitches burst. Once again, she recovered, but my life changed. Suddenly, she needed a lot more help, and because I was the oldest daughter, that job fell on me. At nine years old, I felt as if my childhood was over. I learned to put my needs on hold, a habit I still struggle with to this day.

Years later, my caregiving role became complicated when my mother passed away suddenly, and I was put in charge of my ninety-year-old father. At this time, I was running two businesses and working around the clock. Disruptive relatives added a frustrating twist to the situation, and I was forced to set some rigid boundaries.

This period in my life was the hardest, and many times I felt like throwing in the towel. Although I had some support and strong spiritual practices, I found myself drinking two glasses of wine at night and eating all the chocolate I could get my hands on. In addition, there was new drama every day, sometimes caused by the family, other times by Dad. Working seven days a week wasn't helping matters. Eventually, I suffered extreme burnout with a bad attitude to boot.

I didn't like feeling this way, so I mostly kept it to myself. Which meant the problems persisted. Things changed for the better when Dad passed away, but I was a mess from bottling everything up inside. Four long years of caregiving and stress left me with mixed emotions, including bitterness toward the troublemaking relatives.

Untangling those feelings took me almost a full year. For the first time in my life, I wasn't in a caregiver role. I could finally put myself first, something I never did before. I focused on healing myself. Interestingly, I also seemed to attract many clients with similar situations around this period. Tarot was part of my self-care and a way to help others struggling with caring for loved ones.

At the time I am writing this book, I find myself caring for another loved one who is dealing with a serious illness. But this time is different. I've learned my needs must be equally as important as the needs of the person I care for. As the airplane story goes: I must put on my mask before putting one on someone else. The daily wine habit was abolished long ago, although I still enjoy one drink on the weekend. (The chocolate habit stays.) Most importantly, I have self-care practices in place, and the Tarot plays a significant role.

Before we dig into the Tarot, I'd like to offer a few helpful suggestions, beginning with what to say and what not to say to caregivers. These are some of the things I found most beneficial and unhelpful in my own caregiving journey.

What to Say and What Not to Say

What Not to Say:

> You're such a saint! I could never do what you do.

> God only gives us what we can handle.

> I don't know how you do it.

> If you need anything, call me!

> Damn, you look terrible. You should take better care of yourself!

> At least you have help.

What to Say:

> I'm free on Friday. Can I come over and give you a break?

> If you need an ear, I'm here.

> You are doing a great job.

> Let me sit with your mom so you can have some time with your wife and kids.

> You've been spending an awful lot of time at the hospital. I'd love to help out with errands or cleaning. Let me know what day works for you, and I'm there!

The last line is the most important one of all. As I mentioned early, caregivers are not great at asking for help. Anticipate their needs and then do it!

If you're not sure how you might help, here are some simple suggestions:

1. If you don't live close, fly in as often as possible. Tell the caregiver to let you handle things while you're there.

2. Send meals, money, gift cards, or other treats. These gifts show the caregiver they are valued.

3. Offer to pitch in resources to hire help.

4. Allow the caretaker to vent when they need to. After all, it's a hard job, and sometimes a safe place to unload is the greatest gift of all.

Tarot for Better (Healthier) Caregiving

If you're a caregiver, you probably feel guilty if you do anything for yourself. But do you want to be a martyr? Probably not. You deserve to feel safe, grounded, and supported during this time. Let's look at how Tarot can help you.

Caregivers face many issues, from burnout to stressful family dynamics to anxiety about the future. As I said, I've been there, and so have many of my clients. I know what it's like to feel as though you're at the end of your rope and unable to give anything more. Tarot can provide a safe space for reflection, opening the doors for better decisions.

If you're taking care of a loved one, you probably have questions like this:

What is a boundary that I need to set at this time?

How can I take excellent care of myself while also caring for others?

Where can I find help and support so I don't have to carry this alone?

If I continue to give excessively and neglect my health, what is the likely outcome?

What is one positive change I can make right now?

These questions are ones I've asked, and over the years, so have my clients. The first thing you need to do is check in with yourself. I always recommend a daily Tarot draw and the Body Mind Spirit spread, which we visited previously. These simple practices will give you the information you need to see where you are in the present moment and what you need the most. This knowledge will help you make excellent decisions to support you while you're doing the heavy lifting.

Here is a Body Mind Spirit spread I did for myself when things felt overwhelming. At that time, I had to make a painful decision to take away Dad's keys and move him in with a relative. He had fallen a lot and had got caught driving on the wrong side of the street more than once. It was time for him to be in a safe space before he hurt himself . . . or someone else.

Needless to say, he was not happy, and a few relatives balked at this decision. They came up with expensive and foolish options, none of which made sense. These suggestions created intense pressure on me, and that led to heated arguments. One day, after another round of fighting, I came home feeling defeated. I sat at my Tarot table and began shuffling. Here are the cards I pulled along with my notes:

Body: The Emperor reversed—If there was ever a card that showed someone feeling old, tired, and busted, it was this one. I'm sick of trying to hold this all together. My body is exhausted, and I have little energy to give to this situation. I am aware that I'm not taking care of myself. My daily structures and routines are becoming lost in the shuffle. I'm also choosing unhealthy coping mechanisms, namely wine. While it relieves my stress to some degree, I know this isn't actually helping me . . . or Dad. My body feels bloated and sluggish, certainly not like an "Emperor."

Mind: Three of Wands—Although things are hard, I know this is not forever. There is an end in sight. It may be sooner than I can believe. I will remain focused on getting him to the finish line with support and safely, even if X and Y try to stir things up. I will not let them push me over the edge.

Spirit: Death reversed—Another Major Arcana reversed. Well, this makes sense, because my spiritual life is in limbo. I have less time to devote to that. It's "dead" for the moment. But maybe this is the problem with how I am feeling. Perhaps if I find a way to resurrect a few practices, I can create balance. Lord knows my attitude isn't good now.

Looking back, I can see those two Majors as big red flags. I was not in a good space, even though mentally, I seemed to be holding it together. My routines, both physically and spiritually, were no longer a priority. It's a surprise I was even operational!

After this reading, I made a few changes to my schedule. I stopped teaching on the weekends and limited the number of clients I would see during the week. Instead of working around the clock, I had time for walks and rest. Life was still hard for another year, but at least I was functioning somewhat better.

Here's another sample reading: Zara has been caring for their partner, who is dealing with a terminal illness. Unfortunately, they don't have any help because they are estranged from their family. Here are the cards they pulled:

Body: Two of Wands—This card shows a robust and sturdy body. Zara is committed to their fitness and has made recent changes so they can work out at home. They are also making good nutrition decisions for themselves and their partner.

Mind: Four of Pentacles—Another solid card. Zara has everything under control and doesn't seem to mind holding down the fort! They also work from home, which allows them to be closer to their partner, creating peace of mind. Zara said they get stronger when under pressure due to past military training. Whatever the case may be, this is a fantastic card to see.

Spirit: Three of Cups reversed—Zara is not getting enough social activity. They rarely get out between caring for their partner and working from home. While they said this lack of activity doesn't bother them, I felt this card pointed out a need for some fun to blow off steam. I recommended scheduling a day to see old pals from time to time outside of the home.

As you can see, this check-in reveals a lot. The Body Mind Spirit spread should be your first stop if you are in the caretaker role.

📩 **Practice:** If there are multiple people involved in a caretaking situation, each person can do a daily Body Mind Spirit spread and check-in with the other caregivers. This is a wonderful way to make sure everyone is communicating about the situation and their needs. After all, if the team is working together in a healthy way, everyone benefits, including the person needing assistance.

Boundaries Spread

One of the hardest things for caregivers to manage is boundaries. Not just with family, but sometimes with other helpers or the person they are caring for. Learning to recognize boundary breaches and manage them empowers the caregiver so they can continue doing the sacred work they need to do.

Use this simple Boundaries spread when you feel your boundaries need shoring up, or just to check in and see how you're doing on that front.

Shuffle the cards thoroughly. When you feel ready, put the deck facedown in front of you. Cut it three times and then put the cards back into one pile. Gently fan them out and intuitively draw one card for each position:

Card 1: What do I need to know about my boundaries with _____ at this time? (For situations that are general and not tied to a specific person, you could also simply state, "What do I need to know about my boundaries?")

Card 2: What is preventing me from setting good boundaries?

Card 3: How can I care for my needs in a healthy, happy way?

Card 4: What boundaries can I set right now to empower me in this situation?

Here's a sample: Will lives with his elderly mother and is her primary caregiver. His brother Seamus drops by occasionally and spends the entire time criticizing Will. Seamus thinks that they should hire help and that Will should get a job instead of tending to mom. Finally, Will is fed up but doesn't say much because he doesn't want to upset his mother, who feels caught in the middle.

Card 1: What do I need to know about my boundaries with Seamus now? Page of Swords reversed—Will is the younger brother, and there is a ten-year age difference. The dynamic is skewed because Seamus sees Will as a kid, even though they are both middle-aged men. Will has trouble asserting himself because he looks up to Seamus and doesn't want to disappoint him. Will also doesn't like to fight because he feels his brother always has the upper hand.

Card 2: What is preventing me from setting good boundaries? Five of Wands—The biggest problem here is Will's reluctance to get into drama. He's allowing Seamus to push him around, and even though it's making him mad, his fear of conflict forces him to feel as if he has to grin and bear it.

Card 3: How can I take care of my needs in a healthy, happy way? Death—A significant change must happen. It may be time for Will and Seamus to have a serious sit-down. Seamus needs to remember he's not in charge of this situation; Will is. New rules may need to be established so that Seamus doesn't drop by unexpectedly, which upsets Mom. These rules could transform the case and help both men build a stronger relationship, benefiting everybody.

Card 4: What boundaries can I set right now to empower me in this situation? The World—Again, Will needs strict rules to protect the energy of the home, his mother, and himself. The World has a figure surrounded by a wreath, a symbol of protection. The more firm Will is, the more likely they'll find peace.

These two brothers did manage to negotiate new boundaries. Things are better, but not perfect. Seamus still likes to play boss sometimes, but this is the ideal way for Will to practice being assertive.

👁 **Pro tip:** If multiple family members are involved in a difficult caregiving situation, I do not recommend doing readings for all of them. Doing multiple family readings can create a conflict of interest for the reader or a climate of distrust if some of these people try to use Tarot to spy on the others. It's best for everyone to have their own reader.

Finding Support

In many cases, caregivers struggle to get assistance. There are many reasons for this. Some don't like to receive help, whereas others may not have access to a support system. Sometimes other family members get in the way because they don't want anyone else in the picture. In many cases, the burden gets put on one person.

I know finding support was one of my biggest challenges when caring for my father. Sometimes I didn't allow other people to assist me. Partly, I didn't trust anyone to do the job as well as I did. So I resigned myself to my fate, sucked it up, and felt miserable. When I finally did get help from my younger brother and his wife, things felt better.

How can Tarot help a caregiver find support? By comparing options. It's straightforward: begin by considering all the things you might need at this time. Then pull a card for each option and see what stands out. This example spread below uses three cards; you could you four, or as many as you need given what options you want to consider. In the example that follows I've used the options of "a helper," "a day off," and a "a massage." These card positions can mean anything you want. More sleep? Help with the bills? In addition, each position can give rise to subsequent card pulls. For example, the first card below, a helper, shows up as Justice—help is on the way! But who? Perhaps pulling another three cards will help you clarify whether you need family help, friend help, or professional help.

What Do I Need? Spread

Here's an example of a spread I did recently when I was helping a loved one recover from an accident.

A helper: Justice. Having someone else lift some of the burdens will bring balance into the situation. I cannot do it all, even though I assume I'm strong, and this situation is much different than other caregiving duties in the past. Having additional hands on deck will allow me to handle the primary duties with equanimity.

A day off: Two of Cups. Yes, please! Adding some play into my life is just what I need. It doesn't need to be extravagant; even a dinner with a friend will feel like a happy escape.

A massage: Temperance. I'm struck by the water flowing in the cups between the angel's hands. Massage always gets my energy moving in the right direction. I know this will restore my sense of balance.

How interesting that all the cards had an element of balance in the message. Guess it's time for me to hire help, play hooky, and put a massage on the calendar!

Try this one out the next time stress is getting to you!

Common Sixth Sense: If a loved one is playing the primary caregiver role, you don't need to pull Tarot cards to figure out what they need. Anticipate how you might be best able to help and then do it. You don't need to ask them to spell it out either. That puts the burden on them, and because most caregivers are not good at asking for help, they'll probably downplay their needs.

Remember: It's hard to care for someone. Showing you care will help the caregiver cope.

Three Things, Right Now Spread

When life is overwhelming, I find it's easy to focus on small steps. But three simple things can make a huge difference instead of doing a complete overhaul, especially when you have too many responsibilities and not enough breathing room.

Three Things, Right Now focuses on three ways to create ease. Here's the spread:

Card 1: What is one thing I can take off my plate right now?

Card 2: What is one habit I can change right now?

Card 3: What is one kind thing I can do for myself right now?

Here is a sample of that spread I did in mid-2020 when I was on the crest of a massive flameout due to overwork and a new caretaking situation.

Card 1: What is one thing I can take off my plate right now? Ace of Pentacles reversed—Some aspect of my work needs to go. This reversal feels like a hand letting go of a coin; a stream of income may need to be pared down or released entirely. I need quality time so I can breathe.

Card 2: What is one habit I can change right now? The Devil—Oof. I know precisely what this is—wine! I always turn to wine and sugary things when I'm under stress. While they make me feel better temporarily, I also know they contribute to my extra weight and an overall feeling of sluggishness.

Card 3: What is one kind thing I can do for myself right now? Knight of Wands—Putting myself first. In general, anything I do for me right now will benefit my situation and my mental health. I think it might be time for a day spent at the spa or perhaps enjoying a quiet solo lunch date at the local foodie hotspot.

Shortly after this reading, I decided to stop reading Tarot for the public. I wanted more time to focus on my loved one and on writing. This decision was scary because I've been doing this for over thirty years, but it was one of the best choices ever. Suddenly, I had actual breathing room, which allowed my creativity to flourish.

Getting rid of the wine habit took a bit longer. Even though I knew it wasn't doing anything for me, I was reluctant to say goodbye. The Devil card, indeed! But once I finally broke up with wine, I felt much better . . . and found healthier ways to deal with my stress.

Practice: Try doing this reading every day for a week or a month. Notice if patterns are coming up again and again for you. If different things show up, let them go. See how much energy you can free up by using this spread.

Here's another example: Mimi was in charge of her elderly parents. She was the only child, so their care fell on her. Her days were filled with running to the office to deal with nonstop clients; on to her parents' home to cook, clean, and make sure they took their meds; and then back home to cook for her family, clean, and help her child study. This routine had gone on for years, and although Mimi felt resentful, she couldn't seem to get rid of anything that might make her life easier. She wanted to do right by her family and succeed at her job, yet she felt guilty every time she made herself a priority. The Three Things, Right Now spread helped her to slowly change her life in small ways.

Mimi's reading is on page 130.

Card 1: What is one thing I can take off my plate right now? Three of Pentacles reversed—Mimi spends a lot of time at the office. Perhaps she can work from home one day a week or ask the team to take on more responsibilities so that her workload lifts. This approach could add balance to her day.

Card 2: What is one habit I can change right now? The World—While Mimi's drive is impressive, her concern with success is causing her to take on too much at work and home. While it's great to be successful at everything you do, that success can come with a price. This doesn't mean she has to lower her standards; instead, she needs to realize that she doesn't have to be perfect all the time.

Card 3: What is one kind thing I can do for myself right now? Empress reversed—One day a week for self-care and pleasure will restore her sense of balance and help her remain centered in her role as caregiver and mother. The more she nurtures herself, the better she'll be able to care for the people she loves.

Putting yourself first is never easy when you're in charge of other people who cannot care for themselves. But when you begin making self-care a priority, something magical happens: you become more resilient and compassionate. Because strength and love start with giving back to yourself.

Save the Drama for Your Mama—Or Not

In an ideal situation, loved ones come together to support the ill person and the primary caregiver(s) lovingly. But I know from my experience and clients that this is not always the case. Sadly, the stress of dealing with a sick family member can sometimes bring out the worst in other people.

As I wrote earlier, when caring for my father, I was in constant war with a few family members who didn't like my decisions. Naturally, their suggestions were expensive, outdated, or unrealistic. One of the reasons Dad wanted me to handle his affairs was that he knew they'd be irresponsible with money. I'm the most pragmatic one in the family and am fiscally conservative. The opposite of the others.

My father was no angel in this situation either. Sometimes he would go behind my back and sabotage me by complaining to others who saw this behavior as "proof" that I shouldn't be in charge. The stress was unbelievable, and in the end, I had to permanently cut off one of these family members.

My story is not unique. Many families go through the same thing . . . or worse.

So how can Tarot help us find peace when drama seems to be the rule of law rather than some random event?

The Situation, What You Need to Know, and Advice Spread

Frankly, Tarot cannot solve family dynamics. But it can guide you to move through these situations with as much grace as possible. One of the spreads I used a lot during this time is The Situation, What You Need to Know, and Advice.

I created this spread many moons ago, and I've mentioned it in my previous books. It shows you how things stand, as well as the aspects that may be hidden or that you're ignoring; plus, it offers advice.

Here is one of the spreads I did when I found out a family member rifled through Dad's possessions to spy on how he was handling his money.

The Situation: Knight of Swords reversed. As soon as I see this card, I think: this is an act of war. One person is leading the charge and trying to stir up trouble. They are coming with swords blazing and a desire to fight what they think is the good fight. This is the "hero" rushing in to "save the day," only there is no day to save.

What You Need to Know: Seven of Cups. There is a lot of confusion around this. Perhaps they have heard some conflicting statements from Dad, and that's what's giving them the impetus to behave this way. Or maybe they are confused by what they found when they went through his paperwork. Either way, this card shows something isn't clear—although I think their agenda is pretty obvious!

Advice: Five of Wands. Fight back. Do not let this happen again. Enlist other people to help the situation if necessary. If they want a war, I need to make sure it's less easy to start one. If there was ever a card that said stand tall and push back, this is the one.

After this reading, my brother and I decided to make sure Dad was never left alone again. We also put his private papers away so no one could access them. This was the right decision, and it created a lot of peace as the caregiving journey began to wind down. I'm glad Tarot advised me to gather the troops against the snoops!

Here's another sample: Emily is the main caregiver for their disabled mother. The drama they experience isn't from the other family members, but from their mother. She complains all the time to anyone who will listen. If out in public, the mother will holler and cry, and this behavior causes people to think Emily isn't providing the proper care. Their mother bitches to the doctors and will spend hours online sending emails to other family members about how she is being mistreated, which is untrue. Emily is loving, and their nursing assistant training means they know how to care for their mother. Sometimes Emily wonders if their mother is a narcissist.

At their wit's end, they consulted Tarot asking the question: how can I better cope with my mother?

The Situation: The Star. Emily knows they are doing a great job. They care a lot and provide their mother the best possible situation. Also, Emily is transparent about what they are doing, which is why the doctors know the complaints are not valid. This says that everything is done with love and compassion. There is no agenda or abuse.

What You Need to Know: Eight of Wands. No matter how much the mother complains, this card says Emily is on the right track, period. They are moving in the right direction and can continue on as they are.

Advice: Judgement. Emily must trust their judgement in this situation and remain transparent with all concerned parties. Regular announcements to the doctors or family keep everyone in the loop and prevent their mother from distorting the truth. Emily also needs to remember that their mother may be seeking attention. If they can find positive ways for the mother to get that, perhaps she will change her ways. Even if she doesn't, this method could provide enough distraction to keep some of the drama from getting out of hand.

📇 **Practice:** While this is my go-to all-purpose spread for problem solving, sometimes you might find that you need a bit more info. In those cases, I recommend pulling a clarifying card for additional guidance. Feel free to do this but refrain from drawing more than one. Too many clarifiers and you'll get muddled results.

Ritual . . . .

The Anxiety Box. If you are in the caregiving role, no doubt you are dealing with a lot of stress. When I was taking care of my dad, I was so tense that my sleep got completely derailed. I would lie awake, worrying about him and stewing about my troublemaking relatives. One thing that helped me was an "anxiety box." I purchased a small wooden box with a lid and began writing my worries on slips of paper. I folded them up and tossed them into the box. Shutting the lid symbolized putting my worries to rest so I could sleep. Once the box became full, I would tear the papers into tiny pieces and flush them down the toilet while saying out loud, "I choose to let it all go." (Needless to say, that box got full a lot during that time!) Try this one out and see how much better you feel.

Breathwork/Meditation . . . .

If you're a caregiver, you need to give yourself as much love and grace as possible. The Loving-Kindness Meditation is one of my favorite ways to send compassion to yourself.

Here's what to do: Sit or lie down in a comfortable position. Close your eyes and begin following your breath in and out. When you feel yourself beginning to settle down, say this mantra silently to yourself:

On the inhale: "May I be free from suffering."

On the exhale: "May I be at peace."

Repeat this meditation a few times. As you state those mantras, visualize yourself surrounded with loving, golden light. When you're ready, open your eyes. Now go about your day and remember to be extra kind to yourself. You deserve it.

Caregiving can be a beautiful thing. But sometimes it's not. Tarot can help you cope, but don't forget other things: therapy, regular massages, staying hydrated, and time off. When the caregiver is cared for, it's much easier to remain grounded for the important work that needs to be done.

GOOD GRIEF

Grief is not a sign that you're unwell or unevolved. It's a sign that love has been part of your life, and that you want love to continue, even here.

—MEGAN DEVINE

WE DON'T LIKE TO DISCUSS GRIEF in our culture. When someone is deep in the throes of grief, we often feel awkward, fumble, and worry about saying the wrong thing.

We avoid the subject entirely or tiptoe around it, using euphemisms and platitudes like "God has a plan" or "He's in a better place now."

We tell colleagues, "Take all the time you need to heal," but what we really mean is, "You can have three days off to attend the funeral, and then we expect you back and functioning at full capacity, and we'll never discuss this again."

Basically, our culture is pretty dysfunctional when it comes to grief. So it's no wonder that so many people struggle to process grief and get stuck—grieving for years and years, trapped in time, not moving forward, not really dying, but not really living either.

Because we live in a culture that views death as a fearful process, we try to prolong the body as long as possible, but once the person passes on, we want to hurry up and get on with the business of living. Isn't that odd? It makes no sense to me.

Instead, it's vital we feel what we are feeling and allow others to process their grief in a way that makes sense for them. There is no right or wrong way to move through grief. Some folks get over it quickly, whereas others hang on for the rest of their lives. Others aren't even sure they are grieving.

When my mother passed away, I was instantly thrust into the caregiver role for my father. He was lost without her, which meant I had to focus on helping him instead of dealing with my own feelings. (Not smart.)

I'll never forget the day I arrived at his house with a bunch of cleaning supplies and groceries. He was napping, so I let him sleep while I busied myself in the kitchen making dinner. Suddenly, he emerged with a big smile. "Hello, Marge," he said.

That was my mother's name.

He quickly realized I was not her and said, "Oh . . . it's you." The tone of disappointment was heartbreaking, but harder still was watching his eyes well up. I almost lost it at that moment, but instead, I remained stoic and told him it was okay, I was there, and he was in good hands. He remained weepy the rest of the day, but I didn't shed a tear. I thought he needed me to be strong.

When I left his house, I turned on the radio, Lou Reed's "Perfect Day" came on, and I burst into tears. I cried all the way home. This was one of the only times I had allowed myself to feel sad. I still can't listen to that song without bawling because it reminds me of this time.

I was so checked out during this period that I didn't even realize I was depressed until almost a year after my mom was gone. My days were too busy trying to run my businesses and care for my dad to even notice what I might be feeling. But I remember pounding the treadmill one gloomy day when a strange but familiar sensation bubbled up in my chest. It was a fleeting moment of joy, something I had forgotten amid too many responsibilities. The universe was letting me know that something wasn't right with how I was dealing with my grief . . . or not dealing with it, as the case was.

It took a long time before I untangled the complicated feelings I was stifling at that time. My spiritual practices and Tarot helped me move through my grief. Neither were silver bullets, because grief moves at its own pace, and sometimes that can be a slow gait. Frankly, I still have sad moments when I think about my parents or friends who have passed on over the years.

My story isn't unique. So many other people I've worked with over the years have told me about "checking out" or "being the strong one." Some of these folks had breakdowns later on, while others had breakthroughs. Still, others were able to ask for and receive the right kind of support but still struggled.

There may be similar experiences, but there is no one way to grieve.

When it comes to grieving, Tarot can be part of your self-care. I found it to be helpful for me . . . and the many clients who have also lost loved ones.

The Different Ways We Grieve

As I said before, people deal with loss in their own unique ways. You might be private, loud, weepy, stoic, angry, resentful, depressed, or riddled with guilt. You may move through all of these emotions. You may not feel anything. You may also mourn differently for different people. For example, the loss of my mother was profound, but I couldn't process those feelings because I was responsible for my father. When he passed away, I barely shed a tear. Truthfully, I was relieved because caring for him while battling various family members was stressful.

Remember that situations are unique, and depending on the dynamics with the person who passed on, you could have many complex emotions to work through. Therefore, do not judge yourself for anything you may be feeling. By that same token, do not judge anyone else going through the process in whatever way is right for them. After all, there is no textbook on how to grieve.

I'll never forget after my mother died; I went over to Dad's house to gather things for the funeral. My siblings and their partners were sitting there with sour faces. I had no time for their drama, so I busied myself getting Mom's belongings in order: a dress, jewelry, and lipstick she liked to wear. Once I had everything I needed, I was off to the undertaker.

My siblings decided I was "cold" because I "didn't come in and hug Dad right away." They didn't understand how uncomfortable their presence made me feel or that I was not demonstrative. Never have been. Their judgmental attitude created unnecessary tension, which forced me to keep my guard up through the funeral.

Sadly, I've talked to many others who experienced backlash for how they grieved . . . or didn't. Suppose you're on the receiving end of this energy. In that case, you'll need to keep your boundaries high to process your emotions safely. But if you're the one who is having a hard time with someone else's behavior, stop yourself. What is this really about? Why do you assume someone should be acting a particular way? Is there a real cause for concern (for example, the person is abusing substances or being nasty)? Or are you projecting your beliefs onto them?

If that is the case, you'll need to mind your own grieving business. Suppose it is the latter, and you witness someone self-harming or engaging in other destructive behaviors. In that case, that is the only time for a sit-down. One person grieving in an unhealthy manner can impact the entire family negatively. Therefore, it's essential to make sure everyone feels secure and safe to work through their grief however they need to—as long as it's healthy.

Before we begin our Tarot exploration, let's talk about a few common-sense things to do when you're grieving and how to support someone else who may be coping with a loss.

When You're Grieving

1. Elevate your self-care. You need to be tender with yourself at this time.

2. Seek professional support. Speak with a therapist or grief counselor. Some hospitals also have chaplains on hand who can provide wise counsel. A licensed practitioner is always the best option if you struggle to move on.

3. Don't expect your grief to have a set timeline. It often comes in waves. For some people, the process moves swiftly, whereas others may need a long time to let go. Still, others feel the grief for the rest of their lives, particularly parents who lose a child.

4. Set boundaries with unsupportive people. Do not surround yourself with folks who judge you. You need to be enveloped with compassion, not judgement.

5. Some people may abandon you during this time. Do not assume this means they are bad people. Remember: not everyone will be comfortable with your feelings. Find people who get you and are there during the hard parts.

6. Do not stuff your feelings. That often leads to poor habits such as self-medicating through substances or junk food. If you find yourself doing that, please seek professional help.

7. Move your body. While it's tempting to zone out in front of the television, this behavior can worsen things. Get up, exercise, walk in nature, do a few yoga stretches, or do whatever makes your body feel good. I have found movement really helps to process feelings.

8. Touch makes a huge difference. Ask for hugs, allow others to hold your hand, and get plenty of massages. The human touch is healing.

9. Finally, journal your feelings. This is one of the ways I was able to process my grief in a healthy way. Tarot and journaling are perfect companions on your healing journey.

How to Support Folks Who Are Grieving

Sometimes you may need to play the supporting role for someone else who is suffering a loss. This is tricky business because grief is uncomfortable, and it can be awkward to be around someone who is depressed. So often, we find ourselves wanting to avoid folks who are struggling. Or we toss platitudes their way and try to change the topic when it gets too touchy.

Let's start off by talking about that. Here are some things you should *never* say to someone who is grieving:

1. He's in a better place.

2. At least she's not suffering any longer.

3. This was God's will.

4. Everything happens for a reason.

5. You'll grow from this.

6. Time heals all wounds.

7. Stay strong! Other people need you to be.

8. It was their time to go.

9. He brought this on himself.

10. Well, at least she lived a long life.

Here are some things to say:

1. I am so sorry for your loss.

2. If you need to talk about this, I'm here.

3. I have Monday afternoons free. Let me come over and give you a hand with _____.

4. There are no good words for this. But do know I care and will be here whenever you need me.

5. I know how much you loved him.

Sometimes simply being present and saying nothing at all is fine too. Although you may feel compelled to say something, quiet support can be a wise path. Allowing someone a safe space to process their feelings is the greatest gift you can give.

Simple Ways to Help Someone Who Is Grieving

1. Offer to run errands or help around the house.

2. Donate money instead of buying flowers if you know the person is struggling financially to cover the funeral costs.

3. Call to check in from time to time. Even if they are not calling much, make sure you let them know you care enough to call. (When I was knee-deep in grief, I rarely returned calls. I just couldn't deal with people-ing. I still appreciated those calls and emails.)

4. If they have children, offer to come over and babysit.

5. Food delivery services are a godsend. Instead of showing up with a casserole nobody wants, certificates for favorite restaurants are not only appreciated but sure to be used.

6. Gift certificates for massages, pedicures, or other self-care are always appreciated. Sometimes grieving people forget to take care of themselves.

These little gestures may not seem like much, but they can make a world of difference to the bereft person.

Tarot for Grieving

Checking in with yourself is always important during the grieving process. Once again, doing a simple daily pull or the Body Mind Spirit spread is the perfect way to reconnect with the present moment.

Every so often, I pull out my old journals and reflect on different periods of my life when grief was a constant companion. There were so many emotions swirling around me—frustration, sorrow, worry, and sometimes regret. The Tarot readings helped me process these emotions. Sometimes the cards offered wise counsel, and other times, they simply reflected my feelings. Again, the readings allowed me to work through those tangled periods at my own pace, in my own way.

That's the beauty of Tarot and journals, for that matter. They both offer a neutral space for reflection without feedback, which opens the door for an honest inner dialogue, the most important one you'll have when grieving.

While I recommend the daily pull and Body Mind Spirit, there are other spreads I have used with myself and my clients to work deeper.

The Grief Spread

I first featured the Grief spread in *Tarot for Troubled Times*, a book I cowrote with Shaheen Miro. This particular layout is based on the five stages of grief, a structure created by Elisabeth Kübler-Ross and David Kessler in their book *On Grief and Grieving*. This is a simple yet profound spread. If you (or someone else) are having a hard time coming to terms with your emotions around loss, try this one.

Shuffle the cards and place them facedown. Cut the deck into five piles. Next, choose one card from the top of each pile for these questions:

Card 1: What do I need to look at right now?

Card 2: What can I learn from my anger?

Card 3: What can I do to find peace with the present moment?

Card 4: What is my sadness trying to tell me?

Card 5: What do I need to accept at this time?

Here is a sample reading: Michael's partner passed away a few months ago. They were together for over twenty years, so the loss has been deeply felt. These are the cards he pulled.

Card 1: What do I need to look at right now? Five of Swords—This card shows two figures mourning while one picks up the swords with a smirk. A cloudy sky creates an ominous feeling. The most important thing for Michael to look at right now is how much pain he is in. He feels as if he's been cheated, creating a lot of anger underneath his sadness.

Card 2: What can I learn from my anger? Knight of Wands—Michael is having trouble expressing anger because he feels it might be viewed as inappropriate. He's trying to be brave for others because he assumes they will be uncomfortable if he shares his true feelings. But that rage needs to come out if Michael wants to heal. He can learn how to express it honestly, which is what this Knight is all about. After he does that, he might discover that sharing difficult emotions doesn't lead to burned bridges. Instead, it can build bridges.

Card 3: What can I do to find peace with the present moment? Nine of Cups—Focus on what's still standing. There are many beautiful memories of Michael's relationship with Jared. Even though he's gone, the stories remain. If Michael can look at that legacy of love, he can find peace. It won't take away his loss, but it can help him appreciate his loving marriage and find contentment.

Card 4: What is my sadness trying to tell me? Four of Pentacles—Jared struggled with a terminal illness for an extended period. Still, even so, Michael didn't feel there was enough time to say goodbye. His sadness alerts him that he is still holding on.

Card 5: What do I need to accept at this time? King of Pentacles reversed—Jared decided to stop treatment, which was hard for Michael to take. But Jared felt it wasn't practical to continue with these regimens, which were ineffective and often left him feeling worse. He wanted to be present and enjoy the time he had left. Michael needs to accept Jared's decision, even though he thinks it took him away much faster.

As you can see, this spread is fantastic for unsnarling feelings. If you are doing this spread with someone else, pause with each card and allow them to say what they feel about the image and how it applies to the question. Let it unfold like a dialogue with you as a sounding board. It could be the first step in helping them to move through their emotions.

👁 **Pro tip:** There will be times when folks have layered, complex emotions around deceased loved ones. For example, the person who is dealing with an abusive loved one who died may struggle with anger, regret, and love. It's important to remain a sounding board, which means you need to refrain from making comments about the departed person. Remember, this is their story, not yours. Your opinions don't belong at the Tarot table in situations like this.

Words Left Unsaid Practice

Over the years, one of the most common things I've heard at the Tarot table is regrets about what people wished they would have said before their loved ones passed away. But, unfortunately, those unsaid words tend to haunt folks for a while, sometimes their entire lives.

This sense of regret can happen for many reasons. Perhaps they were not able to be present at the time of passing. Or maybe the death was sudden, leaving no time for meaningful conversations. Other times, estrangement from the family left one person feeling as if they weren't able to have a proper goodbye.

Those words are often "I forgive you" or "I love you." Sometimes, a confrontation may have been desired, but it never happened. Any of these scenarios can create a lack of closure.

I couldn't be by my mother's side when she died. She had a massive stroke in the middle of the night and could not speak. This made me feel neither one of us could say what we wanted to. I often wonder what conversations we might have had if we had known we were on borrowed time.

I created a reflective practice to help me work through these feelings. Over the years, I have shared it with a few clients who could not get closure because there were things they still needed to say.

Here's the practice: Pull the Five of Cups out of your deck. This will be your significator. A significator is a card that signifies a person or situation. It is usually chosen purposefully, but sometimes it can be a random pull. For this spread, we are deliberately choosing the significator. I think the Five of Cups perfectly symbolizes that feeling of something left unfinished.

Now, shuffle the rest of the cards and ask this question: "What would I say today if I had the chance?"

Put the deck facedown in front of you. Pull one card from the deck. Take a few minutes to study the image on the card. Using that as your prompt, write a letter to your loved one. Let the words flow. Your tears may flow too.

Here's an example from a client:

Card pulled: Ten of Wands reversed.

"Dear Mom. I'm sorry I wasn't an easy child to raise. I know I was hard, and my issues wore you down. I also know you did the best you could. I hope the pain between us has been lifted and you're in a place of peace. You did the heavy lifting, and I never said thank you. Thank you for doing the work, even when I refused to do my part."

Some clients felt this practice brought immediate relief. In contrast, others needed to go through this process multiple times to get all their thoughts out. A few told me they burned the paper after they were done. I think this is an excellent practice. It almost feels like breaking the spell if you choose to do this.

Pro tip: Practices like this one can be triggering. If the querent seems to be overwhelmed, have them stop. Take a few moments to breathe deeply together. Breathing together is a fantastic way to calm anxiety and come back to the present.

Common Sixth Sense: Forgiveness is a touchy subject. Some folks harbor bitterness or anger long after a loved one has passed. In some cases, they never lose those feelings. Unfortunately, too many spiritual people like to push "forgiveness" as the "right thing to do." Oftentimes, this creates guilt and shame. When someone feels forced to forgive, it's neither genuine nor healthy because it is not coming from the heart. If you cannot pardon someone for past transgressions, that's okay. Be ready to show that same grace if you find yourself sitting at the Tarot table with a querent struggling to let go. Everyone gets to where they need to be around this topic in their own time.

The Mediumship Spread

Summer sat at my Tarot table with the usual questions: "Will I meet someone, how do my finances look this year, and what trips might I take?" The reading was clipping along, and it was fun working with her. Each time I turned over a card, I watched her green eyes light up as the corners of her mouth moved from joy to pursed.

As we were coming to a close, I asked if she had any other questions. "I'd like to know about my brother," she said. Then she casually added, "He took his life last year."

I glanced up at her and noticed her face was frozen in a still smile, but tears were forming in the corners of her eyes. "Would you like to see if he has a message for you?"

"You can do that with Tarot?" she asked.

"Yes. There is a spread for that. We always say there is a spread for everything." After choosing significators for Summer and her brother (Queen of Cups, Knight of Cups), I shuffled the rest of the deck. Once I felt ready, I laid out the cards carefully in an inverted pyramid as shown on page 146.

The cards pulled were Three of Wands reversed, Ten of Cups, Four of Wands, Fool reversed, Temperance, Star. The cards showed an unplanned journey that led to a party. "There was a welcome committee waiting for him," I said. "He wants you to know that he did this impulsively and is only now beginning to come to terms with it."

Holding up the Star, I mentioned a rebirth and a new start. Suddenly, she started crying. Big teardrops fell onto the table. "Are you okay?"

"Yes. I just discovered I'm pregnant, so this got to me." We discussed her brother, his life, and the hole he left behind. I pointed at the Temperance card and mentioned he was still with her in an angelic form. She worried he was in a bad place, but once again, my fingers went to the Ten of Cups and Four of Wands. "Nope. His loved ones were waiting for him on the other side."

Significator

Significator

Over the years, one of the biggest requests from grieving clients was a desire to know how their deceased loved ones were doing on the other side. Mediumship readings can bring a sense of closure when no other reading can. A message from the dearly departed can help folks feel at peace . . . even if there were hard feelings or complicated circumstances. By the way, whenever I ask a client, "Do you want to know how they're doing on the other side," I've never had anyone say no.

Although I shy away from calling myself a medium, the truth is I have had experiences of talking with the dead since I was a little girl. Most of this has happened in the dream world when my busy Gemini mind is resting, and spirits have an easier time connecting.

I've dreamed about dead loved ones but also random folks with whom I had only a loose connection. Still, they had messages they wanted me to deliver to their families.

I rarely talk about these experiences publicly because people misunderstand mediumship. They assume it will be spooky, or I have 24/7 access to the other side. (Trust me, spirits have other things to do rather than sit on the phone with me.)

Mediumship is never creepy. Instead, I have always found it to be helpful and healing.

For example, I'll never forget when my friend Dave visited me in my dreams. He passed away from an overdose a few months prior. His death devastated me, and frankly, I am still sad he's gone. In the dream, I was at a crowded house party with strangers. I remember feeling uncomfortable, as if I didn't belong there. Then, suddenly, he emerged with a beer in his hand, much as he would have in real life. He looked amazing. Dave was always a handsome chap, but years of drugs ravaged his chiseled face. In the dream, he looked like the "old" Dave before his addiction spiraled out of control.

We exchanged a hug, and I told him how great he looked. Suddenly, I noticed a woman standing at a stove cooking. She was topless with a black patent mini skirt and boots—exactly his kind of woman. A giant tattoo covered her back. I came closer to read it, and it said "angel." I woke up and knew Dave was in a good place, and his Goth guardian angel was looking out for him.

But what if you cannot remember your dreams? Or if you've never felt the presence of a spirit? This is why I created my Mediumship spread. It's one of my favorites.

The Mediumship Tarot spread can provide information on the departed loved one's journey as well as any messages they want to share. By the way, when I do this spread, I almost feel as if I'm going into a bit of a trance as soon as I begin shuffling the cards. I like to say that shuffling is a ritual act; I'm not the first Tarot reader to say the process of moving those cards in our hands creates an altered state.

We begin with significators: First of all, the Mediumship spread requires the use of significators. As I mentioned in the previous section, a significator is a card deliberately chosen to represent a person (or situation). Most of the time, I use Court cards based on age, gender, and astrology sign.

Here are the significators:

Page: young person or child

Knight: someone who identifies as a young adult male

Queen: someone who identifies as a mature female

King: someone who identifies as a mature male

Each significator will be one of four suits:

Wands: Fire sign (Aries, Leo, Sagittarius)

Cups: Water sign (Cancer, Scorpio, Pisces)

Swords: Air sign (Gemini, Libra, Aquarius)

Pentacles: Earth sign (Taurus, Virgo, Capricorn)

I am a Gemini and identify as a female, so I would choose the Queen of Swords to represent myself. If the Courts don't "speak" to you, feel free to pick a card that does. One of my friends prefers the Magician as his significator. (It fits him like a brand new leather jacket!)

In the mediumship reading, we'll use two significators—one for the querent and one for the deceased.

Here's how to do the reading: Begin by asking the querent what their sign is and how they identify. Then, ask for the deceased person's birthday or sign, along with the gender with which they identify. Depending on the information provided, I will then choose a card for both of them. For example, if I was doing a reading for my friend Dave, who is a fellow Gemini, I would choose the Knight of Swords.

There are circumstances where I'll choose the High Priestess to represent the deceased:

1. If the querent doesn't know their birthdate or sign.

2. If the querent and departed share the identical significator.

3. If the querent is asking about a pet.

The reason why: The High Priestess represents the veil between worlds, so it makes sense to use this card as a significator for the preceding situations. That being said, some folks like to choose a card with a similar animal for readings about pets. I'll leave that up to you.

Shuffle the cards thoroughly. When you feel ready, put the deck facedown, cut it into three piles with your left hand, and put the deck back together.

Now, go through the deck to find the significators. You might wonder, "Why not take them out first?" Good question. The reason is that if the two significators are next to each other, that's a sign that the departed person is with the querent at the time of the reading.

Once you find the significators, pull them out and put the querent's card in position one and the deceased person's card in position two. Then, taking from the top of the deck, lay out the next three cards. They represent the soul's journey. Lay the last three. They represent messages the spirit has for the querent. You'll read the threes as a whole.

Here is a sample spread: After my father passed away, he visited me many times in my dreams. He was always nattily dressed, which made me joke that Dad was probably palling around with Halston on the other side because he was usually in work clothes when he was alive. There came a time when the visits stopped, so I did the Mediumship spread to see what he was up to.

I pulled the Queen of Swords for myself and the King of Pentacles for him. Dad was a Virgo and loved gardening, so it was the perfect significator. The three cards for his journey: the Hanged One, Ace of Swords, and the Lovers. These cards show he was ready to let go, and when the time came, it was swift. The Ace of Swords made me think of his last breath and the cutting of ties from his earthly body. It also felt like his journey was a "breakthrough" for him. The Lovers assured me he was in a beautiful place with his beloved, my mother.

The three cards for the message were the Tower, Five of Cups, and Queen of Wands. My mother was a Sagittarius—the Queen of Wands! When she passed away, my father was lost without her. These three cards reflected that. Her death turned his life upside down, and he never stopped grieving. But now he's with her and wanted me to know he is where he wanted to be.

This reading moved me so much that I kept it in a diary and use it whenever I teach the spread.

Some general rules: The Devil does not mean someone is in hell. It means they are having difficulty letting go of their loved ones here on earth. They are still "bound." So when this card shows up, I instruct the querent to do a ritual to release the spirit. A simple candle burning usually works wonders. If they are Catholic, I recommend having nine masses said for the departed one. (I did that for my parents because they were staunch Catholics.)

Certain cards represent guardian angels: the Lovers, Temperance, the World, the Wheel of Fortune, Strength, the Star. If any of these cards come up, it might mean the deceased person is playing the guardian angel role for the querent, or the departed is with their guardian angel.

Suppose so-called scary cards emerge, like the Ten of Swords. In that case, this is usually an indicator that the spirit was feeling scared about letting go. Their transition may have been challenging.

Spirits never give angry messages. EVER. It's always about love, love, love.

If there are a lot of Court cards, they usually represent other folks who have passed on before the spirit. Sometimes, this reading can lead to rich conversations about other family members who have been long gone.

The Ten of Cups, Three of Cups, Ten of Pentacles, and Four of Wands show a welcoming committee waiting on the other side.

Judgement can symbolize preparing for rebirth. For people who have lost a child, it can signify that the child's spirit is still with them.

For questions about pets, look for cards with animals. For example, if you're reading about a dog, and the Fool shows up, that is a great omen!

Suicide is a touchy subject and often brings a torrent of emotions for the querent. Often, they are afraid the loved one is in hell or something worse. However, I have never found that to be the case. Instead, they are usually surrounded by love on the other side. (Remember: people who have suicidal thoughts are dealing with mental health issues. They need compassion, not condemnation. This is not the time for projecting fear-based readings or passing judgement.)

If you are dealing with someone who is not religious, they may not be open to the experience. Keep people's beliefs in mind; not everyone is interested in this sort of reading. For example, some people do not believe in an afterlife. If they have that mindset, this reading could still work, but they may not be receptive to the messages.

Here is another sample: Clay's father passed away after a short illness. Clay wanted to know how his dad is doing. Clay is a Virgo, and his dad is a Libra. Because Clay is young (twenty-three) and identifies as male, he chose the Knight of Pentacles. The King of Swords represents his father.

The journey: The first three cards are the King of Pentacles reversed, the Magician, and the Sun. The King of Pentacles reversed seems to suggest that Clay's father felt ready to let go of his physical body (Pentacles are physical in nature). For him, there was little tethering him to the earth. The Magician and Sun show positivity, power, and rebirth. His journey to the other side was positive. He is happy to be out of his body and is no longer struggling.

The message: Justice, Ten of Swords, and the Lovers. A karmic debt has been settled. Even though he felt sad to leave Clay, he is now watching over him and Clay's brother as a guardian angel.

This is a concise interpretation, but you can quickly see how this reads.

Let's do a few more examples.

Amira's uncle Hamza died unexpectedly, which left a hole in her heart. They were close, but the past year was challenging due to his relationship with a woman the family hated. This relationship caused some estrangement, but Amira did her best to keep in touch. She wanted to know how he is doing.

Amira is a Sagittarius and young, so she chose the Page of Wands. Hamza is an Aries, so the King of Wands was his significator.

The journey: Six of Wands, Five of Cups reversed, Page of Pentacles. Hamza made it to the other side swiftly and peacefully. A crowd of angels was by his side when he passed, and there was a grand celebration on the other side. Despite his passing being so fast, he doesn't seem to have any regrets or words left unsaid. There may be some sadness around the woman who caused trouble, but he has put that water under the bridge. He's learning new things as he adapts to his surroundings. Like a student, he is gaining a new perspective on his life and the people he loves.

The message: Queen of Cups, the Moon, King of Pentacles. The presence of two Courts shows Hamza is not alone. His mother and father passed away not long after he did, and it seems they are reunited. In fact, the Moon almost seems to say he's busy helping them to adjust to this new path. Amira doesn't need to worry; there is peace around this situation, and the other side seems to be keeping him occupied.

• • •

Amber had a strained relationship with her grandmother, Judy, her entire life. Judy was critical of everything Amber did, creating many hard feelings. Judy struggled with lung cancer the last few years of her life but never once did she apologize for the hurtful words she constantly directed at Amber. So naturally, Amber has mixed feelings. On the one hand, she wants her grandma to be at peace. On the other, she's still angry about how she was treated.

Amber is a Cancer, so she chose the Page of Cups. Judy is a Capricorn, so her card was the Queen of Pentacles.

The Journey: Judgement, Chariot, Page of Wands. Her journey was fast. The call came, Judy "packed her bags," and off she went. She's already enjoying her new life on the other side. I could see Amber's face starting to fall at this news. But, again, when someone is awful to you, there are mixed feelings and no shame in that.

The message: Five of Cups, Seven of Wands, Nine of Pentacles. The message showed regrets for making Amber struggle. This may be something Judy is trying to deal with at this time. The Nine of Pentacles is a card of completion. These three cards say:

I'm sorry for making your life hard. Notice the numbers are Five, Seven, and Nine. To me, this signals completion or closure. Although Amber didn't get an apology when her grandmother was alive, perhaps she can gain peace knowing Judy feels some remorse.

• • •

Let's do one for a pet. My daughter lost her cat, Peach, a few months ago. She adopted Peach from a shelter, and while the cat seemed healthy, she had FIP, a deadly disease. Saying goodbye to this kitty, which she had only had for less than two years, was crushing. Once my daughter was feeling a bit better, we decided to see what Peach was up to.

Megan is a Leo, so the Queen of Wands is her card (also perfect because there is a cat in the image!). For pets, we chose the High Priestess. (Again, choose any card with an animal if you prefer.)

The journey: Queen of Swords, Ten of Cups, Eight of Wands. Megan had to make the hard decision to put Peach down, and here, the cat says: this was the right, most loving decision. She made it to the rainbow bridge swiftly and didn't suffer. It's never easy to make a decision like that, but this was the best choice for Peach.

The message: Six of Cups, Page of Wands, Nine of Cups. These loving cards show Peach has many good memories of her life with Megan. She felt deeply cared for and spoiled. She wants Megan to remember those good times, especially when feeling sad. They brought each other a lot of joy—something they can both cherish.

Journaling prompts: Write down your favorite memories of your dearly departed loved ones. What was a time when you were doing something together you enjoyed? Were there special holidays you spent together? What is the one piece of wisdom they shared that impacted you deeply? If you could say something to them right now, what would that be?

One More Way to Connect

If you do not want to do the full mediumship reading, you can simply choose one card for each person you'd like to ask about. This approach works well with a large family on the other side.

Here's what you do: Shuffle the cards, close your eyes, and start thinking about your loved ones. Envision them surrounding you with love. Shoot beams of golden energy from your heart to theirs (if you're not a visual person, simply allow a feeling of love to bubble up inside). When ready, put the deck facedown and fan the cards out. Then, think of someone and pull a card. What card did you get? What is this telling you about them? Is there a message they are trying to deliver? Keep an open mind and let your intuition find the answer. Continue pulling cards until you've asked about all the folks you want to.

I love using this practice when I need a quick bit of guidance from my ancestors. For example, today, I wanted to focus on my mother. So, I pulled the King of Swords. Although my mother is a total Queen of Wands, she was known for her wit and sharp tongue. I feel that she's telling me to stay focused and stop dithering. If I want to accomplish this massive to-do list, it won't happen if my head is in the clouds. Sounds just like her!

One more. This time I'm asking for guidance from my father. The Ace of Cups seems to be a message of love pouring out of his heart toward me. I adore seeing this card anytime I ask about the other side. The dove reminds me things are healing in their own way, and love is in abundant supply. Because that's the thing: even though our family may be gone, the legacy of love remains. That love is also constant, even in dysfunctional families like mine.

TALKING TO CHILDREN

Children are often the forgotten grievers.

DAVID KESSLER

G RIEF, LOSS, ILLNESS, AND TRAGEDY are hard for kids to understand, especially when they are small. Any kind of change can be hard for a child. As a result, children are often left out of conversations, especially those conversations about loss. Partly, this is due to our grief-averse society. Also, adults assume children are not emotionally capable of comprehending grief or difficult changes. Sometimes, adults want to protect them from unpleasant things, so the topic is quickly dismissed or discussed only when they are not around.

This behavior is unhealthy because it sweeps children's feelings under the carpet, which sends the message "grief is bad" and "you can't be sad." How can they process their emotions around death when they cannot talk about it?

Tarot can be a wonderful way to open dialogues about grief or other challenging emotions with children. Tarot's rich symbolism is akin to a picture book, which is easy for kids to understand. Here are a few ideas. First, you'll need a kid-appropriate Tarot deck. I recommend *Tarot for Kids*, a deck I created with Kailey Whitman, or an animal-themed one such as *The Cat Tarot* or *The Wild Unknown*. Let the child pick one they like so they feel empowered.

Next, you can have the child go through the deck to find a card or two that sums up how they feel right now. For example, say they choose the Nine of Swords, a card associated with anxiety and sadness. Ask the child what the card means to them and why they chose it. Allow them time to talk while you simply witness. Remain encouraging but refrain from pat answers such as "You'll get over it in time." Instead, let them process whatever is coming up.

The child might choose to pull a few cards. Once again, let them have the floor. This is their time to share, explore, and trust their instincts. You might be surprised at some of the things children share when you open the door to conversations. And once that door is open, *walk through*. Keep the conversation going.

Another tactic is to pick a card that shows how you feel first. Then, begin by telling your child what the card means for you in the situation. This teaches active listening and compassion.

One more thing you can do: have your child randomly pull three cards. Then, ask them to use those cards as a way to tell a story about the person who passed on. Again, this simple practice builds Tarot and storytelling skills while giving the child an opportunity to talk about the departed loved one.

Tender Topics

Although all loss is hard, some losses seem more challenging than others. Loss through suicide, violence, or addiction can be difficult to bear. And sadly these events—and school shootings in particular—are becoming more and more what children see as the norm. Even more devastating is the loss of a child. No parent who experiences this loss will ever get over it. The pain may ease with time, but it doesn't go away. In some cases, the sadness never seems to let up.

In these situations, you need to be extra-tender with yourself or the grieving person. Definitely try some of the readings in this section. But if it seems to be too much, encourage kids to seek support from a grief counselor. Counselors are well equipped to help deal with such tragedies.

• • •

In the next chapter, we will look at how we deal with natural disasters and global tragedies. Keep in mind that these are things that children are also keenly aware of, even if it's not happening directly to them or to their families or friends. We live in a 24/7 cycle of constant "breaking" news. Whether we're directly listening to the news or not—on television, radio, on social media—be aware that for children (who are natural sponges!), this ongoing onslaught of information is ever-present. A friend of mine had a daughter who was 8 years old at the time of 9/11. They lived no where near New York. But the child had a panic attack every time a plane flew over their house. If it could happen in New York, it could crash into their house too, right?

NATIONAL AND GLOBAL TRAGEDIES

Trauma creates change you don't choose. Healing is about creating change you do choose.

MICHELLE ROSENTHAL

'LL NEVER FORGET WHEN 9/11 HAPPENED. The night before, my husband was tense, and we couldn't figure out why. We were tossing cards and examining his astrology chart, but it was difficult to pinpoint what was bothering him. Finally, I decided to put on some music, but as I walked over to the stereo, a painting of the Last Supper flew off the wall and crashed on the floor.

"My grandmother always said if the Last Supper falls, something bad is about to happen!" I exclaimed. Spooked but unsure what that might be, we called it a night and went to bed. The following day, my husband roused me out of bed, and we both watched the television in horror as the second plane hit the second tower.

This shocking event shook the world. My clients canceled that week because they assumed the world was ending. After a bit of time passed, I found myself doing a lot of readings to help people make sense of this tragedy. Frankly, it's hard to comprehend cataclysmic events like this.

The world seems filled with terrible news—mass shootings, wars, pandemics, accidents, and natural disasters—and they affect every one of us on some level. But even if you are not a witness to a tragedy, you can still be emotionally impacted.

Collective grief is real. It leaves folks feeling powerless, angry, or scared. Unfortunately, collective grief can also create a climate of fear, affecting communities, cities, or nations.

So how do we find healing as a community or on a global level after a crisis?

First, it's essential to share your grief with your community. Candlelit vigils are one way. In some cases, marches or demonstrations may be cathartic. If you belong to a spiritual organization, coming together for prayer, meditation, or other activities can be helpful.

It can also be helpful to come together and take action. That might mean creating a drive to raise money for folks who may have been directly affected. Or, in some situations, it might mean contacting representatives and demanding change. This approach feels empowering.

Lastly, it's okay to unplug if the situation is too much. For example, watching the news puts my teeth on edge when a crisis happens. While I want to remain informed, there's something about the newscasters' voices that makes me anxious, so I know it's better for me to read information. Only you can determine how much data you can tolerate. Honor your feelings and create as much breathing room as you need.

Sometimes, a group Tarot reading can be a way to bond over troubled times. Here's how you do that: One person is in charge of shuffling the deck. Once they feel ready, the deck is laid facedown on a table and fanned out. Each person draws a card and uses the imagery as a prompt to discuss the event and how they feel. While they talk, everyone else listens without feedback or advice. Instead, they allow each person to share freely. Once everyone has had a turn, it's time to discuss some of the things that came up. You might discover that most of the folks present feel the same.

Body Mind Spirit Spread for the Collective

The Body Mind Spirit spread isn't limited to individuals. I have found it is also an excellent way of checking in with the collective after a crisis. It can show where healing is happening . . . or needs to. Remember, the needs are always significant after a tragedy in all three categories. The recovery is long because the scars run deep.

Instead of looking at the cards as you would for a person, you would consider a community, city, village, country, or the world. Once again, shuffle the cards thoroughly while focusing on your intent. Are you checking in with a particular community directly affected by the situation, or are you looking at the greater whole? Breathe deeply and put the deck facedown in front of you when you feel ready.

Cut the cards into three piles and put them back any way you like. Then out fan the deck and choose one card for each position. Finally, turn them over and interpret them.

I did a sample spread after the Uvalde school shooting in Texas. In this massacre, a gunman entered an elementary school and murdered nineteen children and two teachers. In this reading, the focus is on the Uvalde community a few weeks after the tragic event.

Body: Seven of Wands—In this reading, the body is the overall well-being of the community. This card shows a struggle. This event is still fresh at the time I'm writing this book, so I am not surprised to see the community is having a hard time getting back on its feet. There is also a lot of conflicting information, so perhaps this card means the people in Uvalde are pushing to get to the truth. However, anger and frustration mount as that information seems to be unforthcoming. The longer people have to wait to find out what happened and what will be done, the harder it will be for the community to heal.

Mind: King of Wands reversed—There is a lot of anger toward weak leadership. The community might be angered at the school, law enforcement, and the government for the way they have handled things so far. Some folks may be calling for new leadership. That might bring some closure.

Spirit: The Magician—The spirit of the people who live in Uvalde is strong. This situation might motivate them to come together for change. Remember: the Magician gathers the tools to manifest a goal. Although this tragedy has left scars that will take a long time to heal, the people are just starting to fight for justice and change.

Notice the prevalence of Wands. Wands symbolize passion and willpower. The people of Uvalde are strong, especially when they work together.

While Tarot cannot erase the pain of global or local tragedies, it can help bring perspective, the first step to healing.

Candlelight Vigils. As I mentioned earlier, candlelight vigils are an excellent way for communities to come together when a tragedy strikes. This is a way for people to share their grief, and it can lead to inspired action. In our book, *Tarot for Troubled Times*, Shaheen Miro and I shared information about creating a vigil. So I thought I might include that piece in this book, too.

Here is what you need to know about creating a candlelight vigil: You may have seen candlelight vigils on the news or perhaps in your neighborhood. In short, these are events where people come together around a cause, injustice, or important anniversary to light candles and show their support. This is often an effective way to spread a message and to offer support, especially after a tragedy.

There is also something quite magical about people coming together in this way. A group of people, standing together in unison with candles lit is a way of not only drawing attention to a cause but also raising the vibration. Think of it as a public ritual for peace.

Here's how to organize your own: Once you're clear on what the focus of your vigil will be, it's time to decide on a date. Your date may be picked for a favorable time of the year, or, in the case of an anniversary, on a specific date.

Next, you'll need to find a public location such as a park, community center, or, in the case of a vigil for justice, in front of a government building such as city hall or the local courthouse. You may also need to decide on an alternate location in the case of inclement weather.

Gather your supplies. You can find inexpensive candles with paper drip protectors online or at your local church supply or hobby store. Make sure you have plenty on hand in case your turnout is large. If you're concerned about safety, you may also want to consider cheap electric tea lights. They can work just as well. If you are making banners and placards, you'll also want to visit a store that sells art supplies. For example, you may want to head down to your local art, stationery, or dollar store for poster board and markers. Get creative here; make signs and banners that will catch attention!

Decide on how your vigil will proceed. Will there be a walk through a neighborhood toward a specific destination? Will there be speakers of any sort? Will there be singing, prayer, or poetry? Or will this be a silent vigil? Be sure to organize your event so that it flows smoothly.

Get the word out by posting your event on social media or contacting your local media. You may also want to hand out flyers around town. Share the news as widely as you can so your vigil is well attended.

The day of the vigil, be sure to arrive early to set things up. You'll want to be as organized as possible so that things can run smoothly. This includes handing out signs and candles or showing people where to go. Once it's time, start out with an introduction, set an intention, and from there, light the candles. Let the magic begin!

In the next chapter, we will explore dying.

TAROT FOR DYING

Grief is the awakening: a sign of life stirring towards itself.

STEPHEN JENKINSON

I THINK ABOUT DEATH A LOT. It might be because I have a Moon in Scorpio and an eighth house stellium (astrology is an all-purpose scapegoat). Or maybe I'm morbidly inclined because I'm a woman of a certain age. After all, my days are getting shorter. But there is another explanation for my fascination with it.

I grew up in a household with a large extended family. My mother came from a family of thirteen, while my dad was one of the younger members in a family of nine. Many of my aunts and uncles had families of five or more. This meant the odds we would attend funerals regularly were pretty good.

I also had a sickly mother, who was in and out of the hospital at various times. Her health kept me in a quiet panic, always worried a shoe would eventually fall to the floor and she'd be gone. But because of this background, I grew comfortable being around bereaved folks. Funerals were never a place of dread; instead, they were an opportunity to see family members I hadn't been around in a while. We could connect over stories of the past and a good meal.

My nature tends to be stoic (also a Scorpio Moon thing), so I am good at being a rock for folks to lean on when tragedy strikes. This was something I learned early on too.

I remember one funeral where a cousin passed away unexpectedly. My mother wasn't close to this person, but she took his death hard. She sobbed uncontrollably at the funeral, which continued well after we left. My father seemed perturbed, so I sat beside her, trying to provide comfort. I was quiet and allowed her to do what she needed without judgement. At this time, I was barely twelve years old. When I think back on how composed I was, I can say this experience set the tone for my career as a Tarot reader.

I know how to be present not only for those who are grieving but also for those who are dying.

Sadly, our culture does not honor dying. Instead, as Stephen Jenkinson says in his book *Die Wise*, we treat it with fear and do what we can to preserve the body. Many of those treatments buy us time, but they don't stop the inevitable: eventually, we will all die. When you stop to consider that fact, it seems pointless to fight it so hard when death comes knocking at the door.

Dying doesn't need to be viewed as a horrible thing. But, unfortunately, too often, it is. Doctors are taught to keep people alive, and sometimes this effort may be fine, but often it prolongs the suffering. In other cultures, death is viewed as something natural. Instead of being sad, death is treated as a celebration.

For example, in Nigeria, the Igbo tribe has two burials—the second being a party with a bull slaughter, drumming, dancing, and poetry to celebrate the ancestors. The Melanesia people don colorful masks to connect with spirits and ancestors. In New Orleans, there is a jazz funeral, where mourners parade through the street on the way to the burial with a brass band by their side. The music begins on a sad note but soon turns to a celebratory beat with people joining the mourners dancing along the street. Some Buddhist cultures see death as a chance for reincarnation. They ensure their relatives have a good incarnation by lighting paper money known as hell and heaven notes.

We all want death to be easy. Most people pray for that. Even I want to be like my uncle, who was watching television with his wife. He asked her to get him some ice cream, and when she returned with his sundae, he was gone, just like that.

Some want to be tranquilized to the point where they feel nothing. My parents were provided morphine, which is common in America. This medication took the pain away, but it didn't stop what was coming.

Other people are not so fortunate. Another uncle died from a painful bowel obstruction. His death was not easy, although it was swift. By the time he got to the hospital, there wasn't anything doctors could do except help him go peacefully.

It's this type of situation or worse that most of us dread. Yet pain is often present at death, just as it is at birth. Many years ago, I watched the movie *Casper* with my children. Christina Ricci played a little girl who was friends with a ghost. She asked him what dying was like. He said, "It's like being born, only backward." That line stuck with me all these years. I still think of death like that, and my experience with my father felt like he truly was going home.

When It's Your Time to Go

Not many of us think about death, but it's crucial we do. After all, it's the one thing every single human will experience at some point. Even though our culture does not like to talk about this part of the journey we call life, the media certainly seems to have plenty of time to advertise life insurance ads! Unfortunately, these ads tend to play on fears of dying—and funeral costs. While they promise peace of mind, I find they elicit anxiety instead.

Instead, meditating on how you want to move through the process of death and having honest conversations with your loved ones will help alleviate some anxiety. I believe this meditation opens the door for a brave exit when you are present, aware, and able to talk openly about your wishes.

For example, when my ex-father-in-law found out his cancer had returned, he decided he didn't want to go through treatment again. He'd had enough of it. Instead, he began actively planning his death, including the environment. He wanted to die in his beautiful home by the lake with his family around him. Those wishes were honored, and he had the perfect send-off. There were no dry eyes—but instead a feeling of closure that only comes when someone faces the end with courage and some measure of control.

I often think about rock star David Bowie, who was sick for some time. He kept his illness under the radar, so when he passed away, the world was shocked. A few days later, his album *Blackstar*, which was about death, dropped. Like a true Capricorn, he had every detail plotted out perfectly. It took me a long time before I listened to that album, but when I was finally able to, I thought it was the ideal tribute to his life and passing.

Common-Sense Pieces of Wisdom

Before we dive into Tarot readings for dying, I wanted to add some practical advice. These are things to think about now before it's too late. But first, a story.

Shortly before my mother passed away, my father asked me to look over their finances. She had always been in charge . . . and was a spendthrift. Many times in the past, I was forced to bail them out and straighten her messes. Judging by his tone, I knew I would be walking into another fiscal disaster. She was furious that he had asked me, which set off additional alarm bells in my head. What was the situation this time?

I soon found out. Not only were they deeper in debt than ever before, but they had no funeral plans and the will wasn't signed. Immediately, I got on this topic, which again made her angry. She claimed I "wanted her to die," but that wasn't the case. I wanted her to die well, which couldn't happen with how things were. I also had to explain to her that I needed to get this business in order, because if something happened to Dad while she was in the hospital, all hell would break loose. That explanation seemed to appease her, so she helped me pick out certain things for her funeral and then seemed relieved it was done.

A few days later, she passed away. Instead of a hot mess funeral, it was calm and orderly, which meant my father could grieve in peace rather than run around making arrangements. While this was a last-minute hustle to the touchdown line, it didn't need to be.

Because we live in a death-averse culture, scenarios like this are common. I've met many people, healthy and not, who have no plans in place. Sometimes it's because they assume they have a lot of time. Other times, it means facing your end, something most of us want to avoid. But if we are conscious and prepared, we can pass peacefully without causing harm or confusion to those we leave behind.

For example, someone I know passed away without signing their will. The estate was sizable, but the lack of signature meant it got hung up in probate court for years. No doubt that person didn't want their children to have to fight it out in the legal system as long as they did. But because they didn't follow through, the situation left behind was painful and stressful for their children.

Over the years, I've talked with clients who didn't set anything up. I've pushed them to take care of their business before it was too late. So do not put off till tomorrow what can bring you peace of mind today.

Because of what I witnessed with my parents and my Scorpio Moon nature, I'm already well prepared. My will is signed and in a trust, which means no probate court for my family to wade through. All of my other papers are also in order, making it easy to access bank and retirement accounts. I'm ultra-clear about what I want for my funeral as well (cremation, funny stories, and a playlist that includes "My Way" by Sid Vicious). Although these preparations may seem morbid, they have given my family and me peace of mind.

If you are dying, here are some things I think you should consider taking care of now to ease your own and your loved ones' stress:

1. Get your will updated and signed. Even if your means are small, a will ensures your wishes will be fulfilled.

2. Speak to a funeral director and make your plans. Make sure your family knows how you want your funeral to proceed.

3. Write out all wishes for your memorial. What pictures will you post? Will you have music playing? Who do you want at your funeral?

4. Make sure your family knows your medical wishes too. You'll want someone in charge of your legal and medical affairs. For example, if you want a DNR (do not resuscitate), be clear and have one person in charge of this—with written instructions in case anyone else wants to object.

5. You might want to consider getting rid of some of your assets while you're still here. For example, my father had a small amount of money tucked away. He gave that to his children a few weeks before he passed and was able to enjoy giving them this money.

6. Make videos or tapes for your loved ones. We did that with Dad, and the video interview he left behind still makes us laugh (he was a character).

7. Spend as much time with your loved ones as possible. Make every moment count.

8. Destress your life in any way you can. Set boundaries with some people, automate bill payments and grocery delivery, hire help to clean the house or care for you, and organize your environment so that everything you need is handy.

9. If you're able to, do the things you've been meaning to get to: read those books on your nightstand, take a road trip with your child, visit the museum, and eat that ice cream sundae with the sprinkles.

10. A few months before he died, my father was smoking up a storm and drinking plenty too. My siblings wanted him to stop. I told them he was over ninety and lucid; if this is what he enjoyed, let him. I believe you should do the things you love, even the naughty stuff, provided you're not being abusive or it's making you feel worse.

You probably wonder why I bothered to include this advice in a book about Tarot. It's because I've witnessed too many people who have not had their affairs in order, and this lack of preparation led to a lot of pain for them and the ones they have left behind. The situation doesn't need to be like this. Instead, we can die well by preparing well. As I always say: be prepared, not scared.

Now let's talk about Tarot.

Tarot, Death, and Popular Culture

In too many movies, Tarot is often portrayed as something scary (see a theme here?). Fortune-teller stereotypes with bandannas and crystal balls pull the Death card and pronounce (with a dramatic flick of the wrist) that the person sitting at the table is about to die.

First of all, this is wrong on so many levels. For one, the Death card rarely means dying. Second, predicting death is tricky and unethical. Unless the client says they are dealing with a terminal situation, it's never right to say, "You're going to die." (Psst, chances are you'll be right . . . one day. Because the odds are 100 percent that everyone passes away eventually. Duh.)

Predicting Death

As I said, predicting death is rare; even rarer, and you may be surprised to hear the Death card is not usually involved. Can the Death card mean the end? Yes, but there needs to be a lot of other supporting cards and even then it's not a guarantee. The readers who try to predict something like this serve no purpose other than to scare folks.

In my experience, the rare times people died unexpectedly after receiving a reading didn't come from "scary" cards. It was usually a bunch of great ones! For example, I did a reading for a middle-aged addict who wanted to get clean. All the cards were fantastic, which made it look as though she would be successful, and her future would be happy. Unfortunately, she passed away from an overdose a few weeks later. Her family was puzzled by her positive reading, but a mediumship reading afterward showed she was happy and no longer struggling.

Another example: a client who had reunited with her philandering husband wanted to know if the marriage would work out. I pulled the Eight of Cups and said it looked as if he might leave again, or she might walk away. She got mad at me and hung up the phone. Then, a few weeks later, she reached out. "Could leaving mean dying? Because my husband passed away in his sleep."

Again, death rarely shows up the way you might imagine. Sometimes it's the best cards that show a "new life."

One time, I was reading for my daughter. At that time, she struggled with her father, who controlled her financial situation. She wanted to get free and become financially independent. The cards were once again favorable, with the Sun making an appearance. We assumed she would get a job, and that would be that. A few weeks later, he died, and she inherited money from him. The cards were right, but not the way we expected. This is why it's tricky to try to predict death.

Sadly, because of how the media portrays Tarot, some people tend to take the topic of Tarot and death in a joking way. I cannot tell you how often I've had people sit down and ask me to predict their death date. They think they are being funny, but I find this question rude and problematic. Rude, because they are obviously skeptical and are trying to prove Tarot is fake. These people wait for the day when they can proclaim I was wrong rather than using their time at the Tarot table to focus on meaningful questions. Problematic, because what if they took a random date and began creating a self-fulfilling prophecy? While I've never met anyone who did that, I have met people who have had negative readings about other situations and took actions that allowed those interpretations to come to life.

For readers, it's irresponsible to attempt to give an exact date of death. For querents, it's irresponsible to ask. It puts the Tarot reader in an uncomfortable and unethical position. Therefore, I recommend never entertaining this line of questioning, whether you are the reader or the one sitting at the Tarot table.

For example, a client I had not seen in a long time came in for a reading a few years ago. She informed me she was about to ask a question I wouldn't like. You know what came next: she wanted to know when she would die. I told her she was right; I didn't like that question. I also informed her this was not a question I would be comfortable reading on. When I asked her why she would ask such a question, she didn't have a good answer for me. "Curiosity, I suppose."

While there is nothing wrong with being curious about such things, this line of questioning does more harm than good. Besides, in most cases, you'll know when it's your time to go, and no Tarot reader can see that with 100 percent precision because they are not you.

Tarot Readings When Time Is Precious

For those who are dealing with a terminal illness or who know the end is coming soon, Tarot can provide comfort. I recommend using the cards to focus on making the most out of the time you have left, addressing practical concerns such as getting your affairs in order, or exploring spiritual topics.

You might be wondering what are good questions to ask Tarot if you're dying? Here are a few I think are helpful:

What do I need to do to make the most of the time I have left?

How can I heal my relationship with _____?

What affairs do I need to get in order?

What is the one thing I can do right now for myself?

How can I create a legacy I'll be proud of?

What arrangements can I make?

What kind of support do I need now and when I'm ready to go?

How can I communicate better about my wishes?

Is there anything I can do now to make my time easier?

What self-care practices will help my transition?

Avoid questions about what the end will be like or death dates. These questions are never helpful and usually create more harm than good. Remember: even in readings about dying, it's best to focus on empowerment, presence, and courage. Doom and gloom have no place at the Tarot table. So instead, keep it real, and you'll set the stage for a loving, profound exit.

Here are a few spreads I feel are helpful for folks who may be getting ready to let go.

Card for the Day Spread

Sometimes it's best to be in the moment rather than looking too far ahead, especially when you or the person sitting at your Tarot table is dealing with a terminal illness. Once again, pulling a card for the day is simple. I recommend focusing on one of these questions:

What is the most meaningful thing I can do today?

How can I make the most out of today?

What magic can I expect today?

These questions are not only helpful, but they move the querent toward living in the moment in a positive, healthy way. Rather than setting the stage for a reading that promises false hope, such as "Will I get better?" these questions keep the querent grounded in reality and taking responsibility for the time they have left.

As an example, say you ask the question, "What is the most meaningful thing I can do today?" and you pull the Hermit. That card might mean spending time alone with your thoughts. If you draw the Five of Wands, this card might suggest pushing back on anything that doesn't feel good. A negative card such as the Ten of Swords might be interpreted as letting go of expectations and resting if you feel in pain.

This sort of guidance can be beneficial. But, most importantly, it keeps you present in the now until it's time to go.

The Situation, What You Need to Know, and Advice Spread

Many practical issues must be dealt with when you are getting ready to pass—for example, writing your will or arranging hospice care. These tasks can feel overwhelming. But the Situation, What You Need to Know, and Advice spread can give gentle guidance, so you remain present and able to deal with things gracefully.

As mentioned previously, I have shared this spread in many of my books because it's useful, pragmatic, and can be used for various situations.

Here are the positions:

The Situation: This card shows where you stand at the moment in your question.

What You Need to Know: This card will illuminate things you might not be seeing—something important during this tender time. Folks dealing with the end of life are often overwhelmed with emotions and to-dos, making it too easy to miss the things you need to see.

Advice: Advice is just that—guidance for moving through your issues with as much wisdom as possible.

Here's a sample spread: Sasha was concerned about making amends with a friend. This person was someone she had betrayed many years before she fell ill. Now that Sasha was facing the end, she wanted to extend an olive branch, yet she was scared.

The Situation: Four of Pentacles—This card can be interpreted in two ways. For one, it can illustrate how hard Sasha is holding on to the position. But it can also indicate protection—that either she or her estranged friend are shielding themselves, perhaps to prevent further harm. While that may sound discouraging, this isn't generally a negative card.

What You Need to Know: Six of Swords—To me, this card symbolizes a regretful transition if she doesn't attempt to reach out. I see the figure in the boat moving on, but they may feel a sense of a lost opportunity. Notice also there are three figures in the boat—a sign that Sasha may have support if she feels anxious.

Advice: Ten of Cups—This card says: reach out. Make an effort. It will go better than you thought. This is the card of the happy reunion. Perhaps the friend will offer support as Sasha makes her inevitable journey to the other side. But even if she doesn't, Sasha will feel a sense of completion, which will help her find peace around this situation.

I never got to find out if they made amends or not because Sasha was gone shortly after. I can only hope the reading provided some courage to reach out and heal this relationship.

Meeting My Guardian Angel Spread

Talking about angels can be a comforting topic. Many people want to know about the afterlife, and some have strong spiritual beliefs about angelic beings. I have a few of my own!

Some folks don't believe in any of that. If you're reading Tarot for somebody who doesn't want to go there, don't push it, even if angels are part of your belief system. I would also say you might want to keep an open mind if you are not a believer, but the person sitting for a reading is one. If you cannot put your feelings or beliefs aside, referring folks to another reader who may be more aligned is best. After all, you don't want to taint a reading with bias, nor do you want to make someone feel denigrated. Neither is helpful.

The Meeting My Guardian Angel spread about guardian angels is a soothing balm for frightened folks or for anyone who wants to connect with their unique guide for any reason.

For this spread, you might want to use an oracle deck or a Tarot deck inspired by angels. My favorite is Radleigh Valentine's *Guardian Angel Messages*. It's gorgeous, true to the Tarot's structure, and has representation.

Remember that your guardian angel may be a loved one or an angelic being. You'll have to use your intuition to determine who they are.

Shuffle the deck, cut it, and pull three cards for each part:

Part 1: What do I need to know about my guardian angel?

Part 2: How can I connect with my guardian angel?

Part 3: What messages does my guardian angel have for me right now?

Here is a spread I did for myself:

Part 1: What do I need to know about my guardian angel? Eight of Pentacles, Seven of Pentacles, King of Pentacles—The energy here is grounded, hard-working, and pragmatic. I see someone who worked hard. Right away, this makes me think of my father. He was a Virgo, so that King of Pentacles makes total sense; plus, he was a workaholic.

Part 2: How can I connect with my guardian angel? The Hanged One, Two of Pentacles, Queen of Wands—This combo means: have faith they are there, remain open, and don't second-guess they are with you. The Queen of Wands is my mother's card. This

reading blew me away, because earlier in this book, she made an appearance in Dad's mediumship reading!

Part 3: What messages does my guardian angel have for me right now? Four of Cups, Seven of Wands, the Hermit—"We're here and know how hard you've struggled. We're watching everything you're doing and are proud of how you're growing. Trust your journey. You're on the right track."

I gotta say that this was precisely the message I needed at the time. It's also lovely to know Mom and Dad are with me and playing some sort of guardian angel tag team. So like them!

Common Sixth Sense: Messages from guardian angels are never negative. Even if you pull hard cards, look for the wisdom and light in them. Angels are always looking out for you, and they never cause fear.

Angels are incredibly comforting to folks who are suffering from a terminal illness or going through any hardship. Try this reading for yourself whenever you need to connect to the angelic forces in your life.

Creating Spreads Through Conversation

Another process that works well with people nearing the end of life is creating spreads on the fly. Here's how it works. When you sit with the querent, I recommend setting aside more time than usual so that they have a safe space to share what's on their mind. People who are dying have many concerns and emotions. Sometimes there is no place where they can talk about these issues without feeling shamed. For example, when they express fear or anger, they are usually met with platitudes such as "You need to be strong" or a pity party. While folks may be well meaning, these types of responses are rarely helpful.

Instead, the dying need to be heard without judgement. Professional Tarot readers are experts at this. After all, we deal with all sorts of gnarly issues. The Tarot table is a sanctuary and a no-judgement zone. We're also tremendously good listeners. Use this time to take notes on their most significant concerns. What are their main questions? Which things seem to be top of their mind? Is there anything they seem hesitant to talk about, but you sense they want to? Pay attention and take it all in.

You may want to have different decks for the querent to choose from. I advise keeping decks with scary imagery out of the rotation at this time because the last thing you want is to instill fear or add to anxiety. An excellent deck to use is *The Connolly Tarot*, which has peaceful pictures. You might find different decks appeal to the querent, such as oracle decks. I would suggest having a variety, so the querent can pick one that resonates.

You'll also want to ensure you are in a calm, centered place. If you have stress in your life, this is not the time to bring it forward. The reading must never be about you in the first place, and especially not now when the querent needs your full attention.

Once the querent has talked about what's on their mind and chosen their deck, it's time to create spontaneous spreads. Using their main questions, you can choose to do one of two things:

1. You can create questions together about those concerns and use those to form a spread. This is a practice I learned from *Choice Centered Tarot* by Gail Fairfield. I often do this with clients for many situations, but it's especially effective for emotionally charged readings.

2. You can simply choose one card for each question.

    Either method works well.

    I advise you to give your perspective but then allow time for the querent to talk about their feelings about the card and the information you're giving them. Then choose a clarifying card if something doesn't make sense or seems upsetting.

    I also recommend asking the querent these questions:

    How does this card make you feel?

What is the image saying to you?

What symbols stand out, and what do they mean to you?

How might you work with this energy?

You might also have them choose cards as possible guidance if they seem bothered by the cards they chose.

You can choose as many cards as you feel you or the querent needs. This is a less structured way of doing Tarot. Still, many other readers also do this for some situations and find it helpful for the querent. Again, the focus is on them, so rigid rules need not apply, especially if they are facing the end.

An example of this method is a conversation with a client named Sue. We decided to pull a card for each concern and use those as jumping-off points for discussions. I advised her to thumb through the deck to find cards that best represented the issues. These would be significators.

The first thing on her mind was money. Sue's medical bills have been astronomical, which forced her to drain her 401K and sell her house. She's worried about paying for the funeral (she has no partner or children—only a niece) or running out of money before the time comes. So she pulled the Five of Cups. "This card looks depressing, which is exactly how I feel right now."

"What symbols are standing out for you?" I asked.

"The cups," she said. "I feel like everything is almost gone. The three spilled cups show wasted energy and loss, while the two standing say there is something left . . . but not much."

"How does this make you feel?"

"Depressed. Worried. I feel like the universe has been unfair to me," she replied. I directed her to choose another card for guidance. She pulled the Empress reversed.

I told her the Empress reversed is also concerned with lack, but she focuses on asking for help. She replenishes the well by caring for herself and letting others support her. This message touched a nerve. "I don't want to be dependent on anyone. I've been on my own for most of my life. The thought of needing someone to care for me is terrifying."

As she continued talking, we could see her real underlying fear was becoming dependent. This is something many people who are dying also fear. She began to shed tears, and I allowed time for her to talk about her anxiety and anger at her health insurance, which provided scanty coverage. "I felt like I was set up for life and then robbed."

"Which card would you pick to describe that?"

She thumbed through the deck and pulled out the Five of Swords. This is my least favorite card in the deck, and Sue is aware of what the card means, so it was easy for her to choose this one. She talked about how the mourning figures were how she felt, and the insurance agency was the smirking man collecting the swords as he walked away. This card represented her giving so much money to insurance over the years only to be left with nothing as they collected the rewards.

I could see real anger rising in her face. She told me she felt bitter, but guilty for not preparing better and for getting angry about this situation. "Pull another card for guidance." So she turned the deck facedown and pulled the Six of Wands. Here, the figure is in the saddle, surrounded by supporters as they head toward a victory. Once again, we started talking about asking for support. I pointed to how the figures supporting the main character were happy and seemed to be celebrating. Might people be willing to help her at this time?

After thinking about it, Sue said she did have friends who offered to be there in any way possible. These were people there during treatment, like Bobbi Jo, who drove her to the hospital every day, or Rose, who was constantly dropping by to help with household chores. These friends were there without Sue asking for a thing. They knew how to be of service. Perhaps letting them know what she needed the most might allow them to give to her in a way that feels good.

We pulled one more card and got the Ace of Cups. "Ask and ye shall receive," I said. This brought a smile to her face, and we finished the session by talking about her "receiving problem," which many folks struggle with. Learning to receive help will bring peace of mind and open the door for greater intimacy and closeness with her loved ones.

Tarot expert James Wells has a similar approach but also has another method that involves allowing the querent to choose cards faceup. The querent can pick cards they are drawn to—or illustrate how they feel about a particular concern. In a blog post titled *Palliative Tarot*, James writes:

> Another way that the consultation could unfold would be to simply invite the
> dying person to look through the face-up tarot pack and sort the cards into piles

that make sense to them according to colours, characters, moods, or actions
depicted in the images. They would take their time creating these categories,
then telling stories about each in turn, allowing both sweet and bitter memories
to emerge. I would ask them honest, open-ended questions about each story
and notice where that takes them then gently summarise what I hear in each tale
so they would know that someone heard them. The process of sharing stories
plus the ability to choose which cards belong together according to personal
preference would again bring in an empowering sense of autonomy about some-
thing in their life. I might pull a card at random at the end of the consultation to
respond to the question, "What does Name most need to hold in hir heart and
mind about all of this?" to help tie together loose ends. (James Wells, "Palliative
Tarot," *Evolutionary Tarot & Circle Ways,* jameswells.wordpress.com, accessed
June 16, 2023)

👁 **Pro tip:** These readings can be extremely emotional for both the querent and the
Tarot reader. Do your best to remain neutral so the reading doesn't become about you.
That being said, there are times when a reading will bring tears all around the table. I've
had that happen a few times, and it turned out to be helpful for the querent to have
someone share their sadness with them.

Common Sixth Sense: Readings like this can stir up a lot of emotions. It's important to
have some solid practices to release the energy when you're done, especially when reading for other people. Running a selenite wand over your aura or taking a warm bath with
Epsom salts is ideal for clearing anything you've picked up.

The Loved Ones Left Behind

One of the concerns dying folks have is the people they are leaving behind. Some Tarot
practitioners frown on reading for people who are not present at the time of the reading.
While I understand the ethical problems this may bring, when someone is beginning to
face the end, they can feel more at peace if they can inquire about anything important to
them, including those left behind.

I ask them to simply pull one card for each family member. Then we can begin a
dialogue about the card images and how they apply to their loved ones.

For example, one of my clients asked about her son, who was struggling with substance abuse. She pulled the Devil, which is associated with addiction. I asked her if she was afraid he would never get sober. She nodded her head. I thought this card was aligned with her fear rather than his ability to get well.

We chose a clarifying card and got the Two of Wands. This is a card of success, which says he might get his act together eventually. The Two of Wands is also about choices, which means there are many paths he can take. Despite the Devil card, he is not without options. I told her she needed to talk to him about this reading. A heart-to-heart about her fears and his future choices could be the catalyst for him to start turning his life around.

The last thing anyone wants to do is leave the world worrying about their family and friends. So whether you're doing a Tarot reading for yourself or someone else, it is perfectly fine to ask these questions because you deserve to feel at peace as you begin your journey to the other side.

Small Tarot Altars

I grew up in a Catholic household. If you did too, I don't have to tell you about the superstitions and rituals we tend to follow, even if we no longer practice the religion. For example, I still like to petition saints with candles and offerings of flowers for special requests. When my parents passed away, I had masses for each of them. I may not be religious, but I still find peace in those rites.

Most spiritual belief systems have customs they follow to support folks who are dying. For example, Tibetan Buddhists read the *Tibetan Book of the Dead*, while Muslims might have the dying person repeat the Shahada. Catholics might choose to have a priest read the last rites. No matter what your belief, rituals can bring peace to the dying person and their family as they say their goodbyes.

Small altars are one way to create a connection to the divine. Tarot can be part of that.

Choose a space to set up your altar. Make sure it's easy for the dying person to see it, especially if they are cognizant. You might have a candle or flowers. Simple is best. Then choose a Tarot card or allow the dying person to pick one they like. I always lean on the Sun, a happy card associated with success, abundance, and rebirth. Temperance, the Star, and Ten of Cups are good ones. What's important is the image is pleasing and soothing.

Another thing you may consider is tucking the card in the casket or before the person gets cremated. Like Buddhist superstitions about burning heaven and hell money, this is a way to send off your loved one with good wishes for the afterlife. I recommend choosing a card that represents what you want them to have in their next life: the Ten of Pentacles is perfect because it shows family, love, home, wealth, and security.

These little touches may seem odd to folks who are not superstitious or ritualistic. Still, I like finding comfort for folks in whatever way possible. Tarot isn't just for divination or conversation; it can also be a portable altar anytime we deal with stressful events.

Stories

Your stories are your legacy. Before my father passed away, I interviewed him and made a video for the family. Dad was a funny guy, and the video is hilarious. But other parts were more sentimental, like when I asked him who he missed the most. If you or your loved one is facing the end, I recommend filming an interview.

Here are a few questions to ask:

What is your fondest childhood memory?

What were some of the biggest changes in the world that you witnessed?

Tell me about your favorite subject in school.

Who was your first love?

What's the most important thing to you?

What's your secret to a happy life?

Who do you miss the most?

What is the one thing you'd do all over again?

How do you want to be remembered?

What's the one story people will talk about you long after you're gone?

You might also want to create a scrapbook with favorite pictures, poems, quotes, and memories of your loved one. Of course, you can create your own too. In fact, this is a lovely creative project and something you can do with the kids or grandkids. If you would like, you can even paste in a few Tarot cards! These videos and scrapbooks will be treasured by the family.

Ritual

Anointing. When my father was dying, I brought blessed oil from Holy Hill, a popular church nestled in the woods of the Kettle Moraine State Forest. I put a dab of oil on my index finger and traced crosses on his forehead, palms, and tops of his feet. I could see the look of comfort on his face as I did this.

If a loved one is in the process of going to the other side, try anointing them. You can use any oil you like and whatever symbol is aligned with your loved one's spiritual beliefs. A circle, pentacle, or cross is fine. For nonreligious people, trace a heart instead. While you do this, you can pray, offer blessings, or state your wishes for their next incarnation.

Another Ritual

This next practice is a simple but effective way to work through fears about death. Get a piece of paper and favorite pen. Begin imagining what your death may be like. Notice what comes up. Do you worry about pain? Being alone at your time to go? Are you scared of not having control? What are some of your biggest fears? If you had to write a movie scene about your death, what might that look like? Answer these questions and write everything down. Be as detailed as possible. You're getting it all out of your system, so to speak. When you feel ready, tear up your answers and burn the paper. Let it go.

You can repeat this ritual as often as you need or want.

Breathwork/Meditation

As I mentioned earlier in this book, belly breathing is calming and centering. It's the best way to get back in your body and in the present moment, even when you don't want to be there. When you are dealing with a terminal illness, it's tempting to medicate and check out. But this simple breathwork can help you be present with your experience, and that can open your heart in surprising ways.

Belly breathing is also something you can do with a dying person if you are attending to them and sense they are uncomfortable or stressed. Sit with them and hold their hand. Touch can be soothing, but if they don't want that, it's okay to refrain. Let them know you are going to be breathing together.

Briefly explain belly breathing: "We are going to take slow, deep breaths together. As you inhale, visualize as if you're taking your breath down into your belly and expanding it. As you exhale, visualize your belly gently deflating. I'll guide you. Let's start by taking in a nice slow breath. . . . " Here, you'll breathe with them.

Next, let them know you're going to exhale together through the mouth and then exhale. Be sure to keep your inhales and exhales audible. That way, they can follow along easily.

This is a practice I've used with yoga students and distressed clients too. I swear by it!

NAVIGATING LIFE'S
HARD PASSAGES

*The secret of change is to focus all of your energy not on fighting the old
but on building the new.*

SOCRATES

WHILE ILLNESS, CAREGIVING, AND GRIEF may test our mettle, other situations can cause tremendous pain too. The loss of a job, the end of a relationship, or aging—any of these experiences can be traumatic. These experiences should not be minimized or treated like something you should just get over. Instead, we need to apply the same level of compassion to ourselves or others who may be dealing with these struggles as we would to someone who is unwell.

For example, I'll never forget when I was going through a messy divorce. I had zero support at the time. My best friend told me I needed to pull myself up by the bootstraps, which left me feeling scared and abandoned.

How different things would have been if I had a circle of love around me then. Instead, I was alone and unprepared to deal with the trauma surrounding that situation. But I did have my trusty Tarot deck. I turned to it repeatedly as I moved through this new chapter. There was a lot of pain, but the cards guided me to see my way to the other side.

This wasn't the first or last time I needed to lean on my cards. But no matter how many twists and turns I've experienced, Tarot has been the reliable Roger, keeping me grounded the entire time.

In this chapter, we'll be covering a handful of challenging situations from a Tarot perspective. These may or may not be part of your life experience. Even so, you may want to apply the advice and spreads to similar ordeals you're enduring. I also encourage you to continue with daily pulls as well as the Body Mind Spirit spread as you move through these turbulent times.

I hope this information will guide you, even if you feel totally lost and alone. I've been where you are. I get it. I'm here to help you get through this—and so is Tarot.

The End of a Relationship

As I mentioned before, I went through a hellacious divorce. Many of my clients have dealt with traumatic breakups too. When a relationship falls apart, moving on may seem impossible. Depending on the circumstances, there may be future issues to contend with too—dividing property, custody arrangements, and more. In some situations, a partner may be unwilling to let go, and this behavior will lead to ongoing drama for both parties.

If you're dealing with a breakup or reading for someone who may be, there are a few things to keep in mind. First, you want to avoid readings that focus on the ex. I've wasted many hours with clients who want to know every detail about what their ex is up to. Those readings were rarely helpful. It's tempting to use Tarot to spy, but this is not wise. For one, it crosses ethical lines. Second, it takes the focus away from the person getting the reading.

Obsessive questions about the ex returning are also harmful because they can create false hope if you're overly invested in hearing the outcome you want . . . or don't want.

So what should you ask about?

In my opinion, the best readings remain centered on the querent's journey. This means you'll want to focus on issues such as moving on, dealing with practical matters, and healing. Questions about the ex's sex life should be discouraged as much as possible. You should know some folks will insist, and you may find yourself in the unfortunate position of entertaining their obsessions. In those cases, you may choose to stop the reading or reframe the questions to put the focus back on the querent.

Here are some great questions:

What can I learn from this breakup?

How did I contribute to the issues, and how can I change?

What is the best thing for me to do right now?

How can we find peace during this period?

What is the one thing I need right now?

If there are kids involved, you may also spend a good portion of the reading focusing on their needs. That's fine, provided the questions are centered around how the querent can best help them during this tender time.

Modified Horseshoe Spread

One of the spreads most useful for breakups is a modified Horseshoe spread. The reason why: It delivers a ton of information that can help move the querent from pain to a new future.

Here is the layout for seven cards:

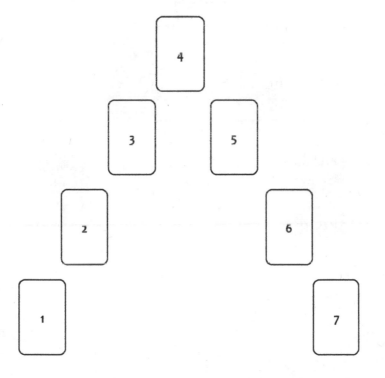

Here are the positions:

Card 1: The past

Card 2: The present

Card 3: The next move

Card 4: Querent

Card 5: The ex

Card 6: Obstacles to overcome

Card 7: Closure

Deanne is in the midst of a separation. She decided to leave her wife because they drifted apart due to conflicting work schedules. Here is her reading of the spread on page 192:

Card 1: The past. Eight of Wands—Deanne began the process a while back. She recently moved out; this card shows she's also moved on.

Card 2: The present. The Hanged One reversed—There is no more waiting. Instead, everything is in motion. Finally, she's standing on her own feet and trusting the decision.

Card 3: The next move. Six of Wands—Although there is pain, Deanne and her partner have good support. This support will give them the help they need to gracefully exit the marriage.

Card 4: Querent. Ten of Wands—Deanne feels stressed. A lot of this stress falls on her because she is the one who made the decision.

Card 5: The ex. Death—Interestingly, the divorce may be an incentive for her ex to make some long-needed life changes. She began planning a cross-country move back home to take care of her mother. Before the divorce, she didn't feel she could do this.

Card 6: Obstacles to overcome. Two of Wands reversed—The physical distance could complicate the plans. They'll need to figure out how to communicate until everything is resolved, including selling the house.

Card 7: Closure. The Fool—This card shows both parties will be free to start new lives. The baggage will be minimal. There is much to look forward to after divorce.

This reading was soothing for Deanne and gave her the information she needed to begin plotting the next steps to sell the house with her soon-to-be ex.

The Modified Horseshoe spread doesn't need to be solely for divorce. You can use it for any relationship that ends.

If a loved one is parting ways with their significant other, here are a few tips on what to say or not.

What to Say:

Now is the time to focus on you.

Let's grab a coffee and catch up. I'm free on Friday.

How are the children doing?

If you want to talk about it, I'm here.

I'm sorry things ended this way.

What Not to Say:

I never liked them.

There are plenty of other fish in the sea.

Maybe you'll get back together one day.

It would be best if you stayed together until the kids were grown.

Being single at this age is going to be complicated.

What if you end up alone?

_____ was such a scumbag (or other derogatory things).

I saw your ex the other day, and guess what they're up to now . . .

It's tempting to bash the ex or gossip about them. But this doesn't do anybody any favors. In fact, it keeps the animosity and sadness going when this situation requires healing. Always aim to support recovery instead of bitterness. With time, even the deepest scars can heal.

Pregnancy Loss

Shortly after I gave birth to my daughter, I was pregnant again. But this time something felt off. I had none of the symptoms other than the missed period. In fact, I didn't feel pregnant at all. But the blood test confirmed that I was expecting, so I tried to ignore my intuition.

A few weeks later, I started bleeding. The doctor examined me and announced I had miscarried. After a D&C, I was sent home. Because my daughter was still a newborn, there was no time to grieve. I had to move on with life, even though I would feel sad from time to time.

Our culture doesn't talk much about miscarriage. It's one of those touchy topics that feel taboo. Most of the time, it's treated like a somewhat smaller loss, one we can move on from like no big deal. The parents are supposed to carry on as if nothing happened and, in some cases, are told they can try again when that may be the last thing they feel like doing.

If you suffered a miscarriage, you know how devastating it can be. Working through grief takes time. In some cases, you may feel that loss forever. It's essential to treat this loss with tenderness.

Tarot can help you reflect on your feelings, which can be instrumental in healing your grief. For example, here is a simple spread for the loss of a child.

The Three R's Spread

Card 1: Release: What do I need to release?

Card 2: Recover: How can I recover?

Card 3: Remember: How do I honor the memory of this child?

After trying for many years, Stacey was elated to be pregnant. Sadly, she miscarried a few weeks later. This is her reading:

Card 1: Release: What do I need to release? Six of Swords—In this card, a couple sails forward with a small child by the shrouded figure's side. When Stacey saw the image, she knew it meant she must find a way to move on from her loss. That doesn't mean forgetting about the child she longed for. Instead, the spirit can travel with her.

Card 2: Recover: How can I recover? Eight of Swords—It's an inside job. Stacey knows that recovering is something that requires time and introspection. She must come to terms with her emotions first.

Card 3: Remember: How do I honor the memory of this child? The Wheel of Fortune—This card is all about cycles. Perhaps she can create a ritual to remember the child she lost. For example, a candle lit on the anniversary of her loss may bring peace.

👁 **Pro tip:** If you are reading for someone who has gone through a situation like a miscarriage, you'll need to be extra gentle. This is a complicated topic requiring a great deal of compassion. Even if you have never been in this position, know that miscarriage brings complex emotions. The last thing you want to do is trigger negative feelings such as guilt. Always treat traumatic situations with care, especially when children are involved.

It's also possible that you'll encounter a querent who wants to ask about an abortion. If they are inquiring as to whether they should or shouldn't do it, that's a question they should take to their doctor instead of the Tarot table. However, if they want a reading about an abortion they had, Tarot can provide a healing and safe space to work out any complex emotions they may be facing. Keep in mind, abortion is a polarizing topic. If you have strong feelings about this issue and cannot be objective, it may be best to refrain from the reading.

If a loved one suffers the loss of a child, you might find yourself uneasy talking about the loss. You may be tempted to brush it aside, but your loved one may need to discuss it. Opening up a conversation can help them process those difficult feelings.

Of course, you'll want to be mindful of how you approach this topic. Here are some suggestions:

What to Say:

I'm so sorry for your loss.

I'm here for you.

Please be as kind to yourself as possible right now.

How can I support you?

I know how much you wanted this child. I'll be thinking of you both and am here to help in any way possible.

What Not to Say:

You're young. You can always have another.

There was probably something wrong.

Maybe you should have/shouldn't have . . .

Some people can't get pregnant; you're lucky you can.

I lost a baby too, but then I was able to have one.

I cannot emphasize this point enough: losing a little one is a terrible thing to go through. This is the time for compassion for the parents, whether that be a loved one or you.

Loss of a Job

Many years ago, I was hired for a bartending job at a new restaurant. Little did I know I was being evaluated alongside a shady male bartender with a bad perm. After a few days, the owners announced I was terminated because they felt he was a stronger candidate. I was furious and humiliated because I didn't realize this was a "dress rehearsal." Luckily, I got another job shortly after, which led to my career as a Tarot professional.

Losing your job sucks, no matter what the circumstances may be. Whether you've royally screwed up or are the victim of downsizing, job loss can lead to stress, anger, and sadness. Fears about finding a new job or running out of money are real.

I've found that folks tend to want to focus on what went wrong and what's next when it comes to job loss. Questions about finding a new job, receiving unemployment, or handling finances are common. So if you're reading for someone else, you might end up covering a variety of concerns.

If you are the one who lost your job, it may be hard to remain objective. Therefore, I have found it's best to have another reader toss the cards for you instead.

Past, Present, and Future Spread

Usually, when people lose a job, they are fixated on finding a new job. Therefore, the classic Past, Present, and Future spread works well.

Here's a sample reading: Jim was terminated from his new job after only eleven months. He was struggling to keep up with the demands; plus he showed up late twice because of complications with daycare. In addition, the boss wasn't sympathetic, which left Jim feeling despondent.

Card 1: Past. Eight of Cups—Jim left another job because he thought the grass was greener on the other side. This move was a step up for him, even though he was going into an entirely new field. He assumed he'd catch on quickly.

Card 2: Present. Nine of Cups—Although he lost his job, he's not in bad shape. His wife has a solid career, and they have money in the bank. This card reminded him that he's not without resources and has room to breathe.

Card 3: Future. Knight of Pentacles—This card indicates an offer is coming soon. It will be a strong opportunity with good income potential. The Knight of Pentacles is on solid ground, indicating that Jim might be heading back into something he knows well.

Jim got a new job four weeks later at a small family-owned company. The pay is excellent, and there is flexibility. Best of all, it's work he enjoys and is aligned with his values.

When someone loses their job, they may feel scared for their future. As a result, they may want to vent. You'll want to give them space to do so, but don't get hung up there. Instead, it's best to turn the conversation to future actions. Here are some things to say and not to say to keep them focused on possibilities rather than regrets.

What to Say:

I'm sorry to hear you lost your job.

I know how hard it can be to lose your job. I'm here if you want to talk about it.

Is there anything I can do to help you at this time?

I heard what happened. Do you want to talk about it?

Let's get together and brainstorm some ideas. I may have a few good leads for you!

What Not to Say:

> *At least you can collect unemployment.*
>
> *At least your partner still has a job!*
>
> *Have you been applying for jobs or sitting around all day?*
>
> *What did you do to get canned?*
>
> *Well, you always did bitch about your job.*

Most of the time, people do move on to new employment. Even so, losing a job can leave lasting scars. If it happens to you, don't beat yourself up. Instead, look at how you can use this situation to motivate.

The Empty Nest

When your child leaves home, there is a mix of joy and sadness. Suddenly, your household is a lot quieter. But it's also a bit lonelier.

The role of a parent is for life, but now you're not defined by play dates and PTA meetings. Instead, you're both on your own. This means you need to adjust to having a lot more time to yourself, even if you're feeling blue every time you take a peek in their old bedroom.

Next, let's look at a simple 4-card spread for reflection.

Now, Soon, Obstacles, The New Beginning Spread

You can use the Now, Soon, Obstacles, The New Beginning spread any time you face a life change.

Card 1: Now

Card 2: Soon

Card 3: Obstacles

Card 4: The new beginning looks like _____.

Jay and Sita devoted their entire life to their only child, Ariya. Now that Ariya is going to college in another state, they face the dreaded empty nest. Sita worries about Ariya being alone, while Jay wonders if being so far away will leave her homesick. Here is their spread:

Card 1: Now. Wheel of Fortune—Ariya is going to her dream school, so this will ultimately be an exciting time for her. Her parents are thrilled she got accepted; they know this is the first step to a successful future. The Wheel shows this being a pivotal and fortunate time, and they should count their blessings.

Card 2: Soon. The Devil—This is a card of fear and possessiveness. Ariya often complains of Sita being controlling, so most likely, this will be an upcoming issue they need to address as a family.

Card 3: Obstacles. Queen of Pentacles—This card faces the Devil, a sign that control will be a big problem for all three. Ariya must remember that they are fearful for her safety, while Sita and Jay need to lighten up and trust her to make her own decisions.

Card 4: The new beginning looks like the Three of Wands. The distance will be good for them. Ariya will learn to be independent, while Sita and Jay will be able to watch her blossom. Of course, they can still travel to be together. But as time goes on, that may be less necessary. Perhaps Jay and Sita can start to explore other travels they have wanted to do for some time but couldn't due to parenting duties.

If your children are leaving home, their leaving can stir up many feelings. But while there may be tears, this is also a time to rejoice. While they are building their futures, you can create a new one for yourself too.

Of course, people can and do say stupid things when a child leaves home. So here's my advice on what to say and not to say to new empty nesters.

What to Say:

What new things are you getting into?

How is your child doing?

Let's grab a coffee and catch up.

We should go out to a concert like old times! It will be fun!

What Not to Say:

Just be glad they're not crashing on your couch until they're thirty!

Are you going to keep their bedroom exactly as is in case they don't make it?

How come they didn't want to stay near you?

I'll bet you're glad to have all this free time.

Remember, no matter how far your kids may go, they are always in your heart.

Aging

I've been blessed with decent health, but turning fifty was a new ball game. I call it the "oh shit years" because I suddenly had issues. Weight gain, arthritis, a wonky knee, not to mention all the dental drama. While I had always intended to grow old gracefully, these developments threw a walking cane into my plans!

Aging is no joke. The loss of youth is devastating, especially if health issues accompany this new phase. But while we may not be able to stay young forever, we can find a way to make peace and embrace getting older.

Coming to terms with aging begins with self-care. As I've gotten older, I found I need to pay more attention to my body, mind, and spirit. Regular exercise, good books, massages, and spiritual practices may not bring back the person I was in my twenties, but it does help me love the person I am becoming.

Reflection on Aging Spread

I do recommend the Body Mind Spirit spread for regular check-ins. But I also love this Reflection on Aging spread I created many years ago after reading a post on the Four Steps of Beauty Mourning.

Here's the spread:

Card 1: What do you need to face about getting older?

Card 2: What is your inner dialogue at this time?

Card 3: What can you appreciate about yourself right now?

Card 4: What are some actions you can take to accept yourself right now?

I revisited this Tarot spread recently. Here's my reading:

Card 1: What do you need to face about getting older? Knight of Wands reversed—Oof. This says: slow down. After my accident, I have been forced to do just that. No more rushing about with arms full of groceries. I need to remember I'm not as nimble as I once was, even though I'd like to believe I am.

Card 2: What is your inner dialogue at this time? King of Swords—I'm logical about this. I know I need to take extra-good care of myself and be more careful. If I can slow down and strengthen my body, I might be able to stay healthy and mobile for the rest of my life (something I've been concerned about since that accident!).

Card 3: What can you appreciate about yourself right now? King of Pentacles—My competence. Over the years, I have accomplished so much. I've built a successful business, renovated my old house, and written many books. I've also guided my two children into becoming compassionate, good people. These accomplishments are something to celebrate.

Card 4: What are some actions you can take to accept yourself right now? Nine of Cups—Focus on what I love to do (write and cook). When I'm loving my life, that's when I feel the best, no matter how old I am or how I look.

After I did this spread, I noticed one thing that was missing: not one word about how I look. Instead, my focus is on how I feel. Ultimately, that's the important thing—feeling great at any age.

If you or your loved ones are mourning the loss of youth, it's not a laughing matter, even though the media like to poke fun at aging. Elderly folks are often the butt of jokes or treated as if they are invisible. Instead, elders should be respected, and getting older should be treated as a rite of passage where experience is a badge of honor.

Here are a few suggestions on what to say to anyone who might be feeling a bit salty about getting older.

What to Say:

You look amazing.

You've accomplished so much.

What new adventures do you have coming up?

I admire you.

You're my inspiration!

What Not to Say:

Just be glad you're still alive!

Once you hit fifty, you become invisible.

That's not age appropriate.

Wow, I would have never guessed you were that old!

Have you considered plastic surgery?

In this chapter, we covered situations you may or may not face. One thing we can all agree on: we will all age. We can't avoid that, but we can treat it with love (and in some cases, a bit of humor) instead of fear.

Ritual . . . .

The Goodbye Ritual. For any loss, saying goodbye can be tricky. A ritual can help with closure. Here's one you can try. You'll need a small candle, a piece of paper, and a fire-safe bowl. Find a quiet space so you can be alone with your thoughts. If you're doing the ritual with a partner, make sure it's somewhere you both feel safe to express your feelings. Next, write a "goodbye letter." Pour your heart out. Hold nothing back, no matter whether you're feeling scared, angry, or sad. When you're finished, fold it up. Next, light the candle in the center of the bowl. Hold the paper over the flame, and once it catches fire, drop it into the bowl and let it burn. Once it is done burning, snuff out the candle. Bury the candle and ashes near a tree.

Breathwork . . . .

Extended exhalation. This breathwork is fantastic for relaxation and also for letting go. Plus, it's easy! Begin by following your breath in and out. Notice the rise and fall of your belly with each inhalation and exhalation. Gradually, begin extending the exhales so that they become slightly longer than your inhales. Keep doing this until the exhale is twice as long as the in breath. After a few minutes, return to normal breathing and notice how you feel.

LIVING WELL

Life is not measured by the number of breaths we take,
but by the moments that take our breath away.

MAYA ANGELOU

S O MUCH OF THIS BOOK is about heavy subjects—some of which people want to avoid. However, illness, caregiving, grief, and dying are all part of the human experience, so we must not brush them under the carpet. After all, while these topics are intense, they can also teach us much about living well.

For example, as my partner and I came to terms with his health issues, we became more aware of the things we no longer wanted to do. I was never comfortable flying around the world, so we decided to travel only if we could drive (Hawaii is the exception). We also wanted to have more time to enjoy quiet activities together, which meant me finishing work at a set time rather than working late into the night. No more events, conferences, or situations that were loud. Frankly, that was never my jam nor his. We chose a quiet life where we could be together as much as possible. While this may sound like our life got smaller, it didn't. Instead, it got more intimate, which suits our introvert natures.

Other folks I know who are also facing the inevitable have begun checking off things on the bucket list. (In case you don't know what that is, it's simply a list of everything you want to do before you die.) This might mean taking up skydiving lessons, renovating the house, retiring early, building homes for the needy, or walking along the Great Wall of China.

For some, attending to their bucket list could also mean getting more involved in their spiritual life. For example, going back to church, joining a meditation group, or engaging in daily practices such as reading sacred scripts could add new meaning to the journey.

Ultimately, living well all comes down to using the time left well.

Buddhist Meditation on Dying

I want to preface this part by saying: I am a wannabe Buddhist (or maybe a lousy one). I've been drawn to Buddhist philosophy for many years, but my formal practice is scanty at best. I just don't have the discipline to sit in meditation all day. Plus, my knees hate it. However, I've taken a few things from my studies that have impacted my life deeply.

Many years ago, I participated in a Buddhist Meditation on dying. Mindfulness of death, also known as *maranasati,* is a way to bring awareness to the possibility that death is inevitable and sometimes unpredictable. When you come to terms with this, you can find great peace.

You don't have to be actively dying to participate in this practice. In fact, you can do this meditation at any time and for multiple purposes. For example, not only to contemplate your own mortality but also if you're anxious about losing a loved one. I have found it to be healing. After all, when you come face to face with something that scares you, it loses its power.

Facing the fact that you and your loved ones will not be around forever has a few benefits. For one, it helps you come to terms with the prospect of loss and death. For another, it allows you to be utterly present in the now. If you don't have forever, why would you waste a single moment on foolish things such as worrying about the latest celebrity gossip (even if it is juicy)? Instead, you'd cherish every second and spend your time in meaningful pursuits. You'd also strengthen your relationships and make more time for those who matter. This is why this meditation is so powerful. Because ultimately, what we do with our time here is the most important thing.

Maranasati is easy to do. First, close your eyes and sit quietly. Then begin following your breath in and out. As you do, contemplate that each breath could be your last. How does that make you feel? What images come to mind? Do you feel like slowing your breath down to give yourself more time? Or does your breath speed up because you feel anxious? Just sit with it and notice every emotion that arises and the quality of your breath. You can choose to do this for a few minutes or much longer. Maybe you prefer to try this practice with a meditation teacher. Find what works and explore the practice with an open mind. Once you are done with the meditation, open your eyes and journal your thoughts.

You can also meditate on the Five Remembrances if you have a busy mind.

The Five Remembrances Spread

Buddha recommended meditating or reciting the Five Remembrances, also known as *Upajjhatthana Sutta*, to remember that life is precious and finite. This practice helps alleviate grasping and attachment. Here is one version of these remembrances:

1. I am of the nature to grow old; there is no way to escape growing old.

2. I am of the nature to have ill health; there is no way to escape having ill health.

3. I am of the nature to die; there is no way to escape death.

4. All that is dear to me and everyone I love are of the nature to change. There is no way to escape being separated from them.

5. My deeds are my closest companions. I am the beneficiary of my deeds. My deeds are the ground on which I stand.

One day, I was repeating these statements to myself when I thought: this would make a good Tarot reading! So here is the spread I created based on the Five Remembrances. The spread:

Card 1: What do I need to know about aging?

Card 2: What do I need to know about health?

Card 3: What do I need to know about dying?

Card 4: What do I need to know about loss?

Card 5: What do I need to know about my karma?

Shuffle your cards thoroughly while thinking about how your life is a gift. Sink into that feeling fully. When ready, put the deck facedown and fan the cards out. Next, you'll pull one card for each question.

Here is a sample spread:

Card 1: What do I need to know about aging? Four of Wands—Getting older is not a cause for despair. Instead, it is a reason to celebrate. Celebrate every day because each day is another chance to get it right. There is no need to fear getting old. Instead, becoming a wise elder is something to rejoice about!

Card 2: What do I need to know about health? Eight of Pentacles—I take good care of myself and am diligent in my efforts. No doubt this is paying off. For my age, I currently enjoy relatively good health. I like to think this is genes and my attention to my well-being. Of course, there are things I can continue to fine-tune about my health, but right now, I can also appreciate how I've stacked the odds in my favor through habits in the past.

Card 3: What do I need to know about dying? Knight of Wands—It's a grand adventure! Really, I do not tend to look at this stage of life through a doom-and-gloom lens. Instead, I see this as a journey to a new frontier that I have never been to before. Often, I wonder if death will take me to another galaxy or an alternative universe. Have you thought about that possibility? It's something I consider all the time. After all, there is so much we don't know about what's out there. Who really knows where we will end up? It's something to ponder for sure.

Card 4: What do I need to know about loss? Ten of Swords. Oof. This is one of the ultimate cards for loss. I have undoubtedly faced a lot of it in my lifetime. Yet, I know there is more to come. Sometimes I worry about losing my partner or my children. I can surely go into that headspace of worst-case scenarios, which is rarely productive. Even though my children are approaching middle age and living fairly risk-free lives, I still worry about them. This is definitely something I need to work on more. Finally, the card shows a sunrise in the background—a symbol of peace after loss or rebirth. This card reminds me that even if I lose a loved one, we will see each other again differently— perhaps on the other side.

Card 5: **What do I need to know about my karma?** The Lovers. The more I love, the more significant impact I'll leave behind. I do work hard to be a good-hearted, loving human. Spreading a message of kindness is something I attempt to do every day. As my friend Alexandra Franzen says, "Be a day maker." Making other people's lives better, even if only for a day, improves my life. This card says my efforts to be compassionate are creating good karma for my next life, but also for here and now.

Practice: Try this spread out. What does it reveal to you? Now do it with a loved one and let that spark a conversation.

Journaling prompt: Before going to bed at night, reflect on the Five Remembrances. Then create a gratitude list for each remembrance: aging, health, dying, loss, karma. For example: "I'm grateful I've made it to the age of fifty-seven. I'm grateful my foot healed. I'm grateful for the time I have left. I'm grateful for my parents who may be gone but still live on. I'm grateful for another chance to get it right every day." Gratitude lists are a wonderful way to remain centered on the blessings in our everyday world, even as we move through difficulties. The Five Remembrances are a perfect prompt for remembering to count everything as a reason to be grateful.

Aparigraha

I'm a long-time practitioner of yoga. (I seem to be better at yoga than Buddhism!) It has benefitted not only my health but also my spiritual life. The philosophy is appealing because it has an excellent foundation based on spiritual principles outlined in the Yoga Sutras.

Impermanence is part of yoga's *Yamas*, which are guidelines for living. In the Yamas, *Aparigraha* means "nonpossession," or the virtue of nongrasping or nongreediness. When you begin to let go, you can become more with the present moment and live your life with an open heart. One of the things I like to say to people is to make a fist. You cannot love with a fist; you can only fight. Open the hand, and you are ready to receive. This is a way of showing we must keep open minds, hearts, and palms. When we let go of thoughts, grudges, people, things, and possessions, we become free. Death frees us too. We are liberated from our bodies and troubles.

Let's pull a card for Aparigraha. Where do I need to practice nongrasping?

The Star—Interesting. The Star is associated with healing, wishing, and visibility. I know that I tend to be uptight through my healing work. When I fell and injured my ankle, I didn't want to accept the fact that I needed to rest if I wanted to heal. I was hung up on my independence, which meant I resisted the healing process I needed to go through. The figure in this card is relaxed, letting water flow. Instead of being in that mindset, I was busy plotting how I could still exercise. I even tried to get up and go to the store right after I injured myself! This stubbornness is unhelpful if I want my body to heal when it's not feeling well.

What about you? Where do you hold on? What needs to go in order to free you? Where can you be less graspy and more open?

Ponder those questions and remember: holding on for dear life doesn't allow for a real life. So let go, let go, let it all go. Just be.

FINAL THOUGHTS

EVERY DAY, I STILL PULL A CARD. It's not that I am looking for the Tarot to tell me what to do, but I'm seeking a way to be utterly present. That daily pull reminds me of where I am and what is possible. It helps me live my life fully instead of sleepwalking through my days.

You'll notice presence plays a big part in this book. The breathwork, meditation, and Tarot practices are centered around being here, right now, no matter what's happening.

Because that is the secret to a life well lived: being present with every moment, no matter whether that moment is filled with joy, sorrow, or other such things. Nothing is permanent, which means we need to make every moment count, from our first breath to our last.

I don't want to miss a thing.

xo

Theresa

ACKNOWLEDGMENTS

Thank you to my Weiser family. I love being on this planet with you all! Special big thanks to Kathryn Sky-Peck, who is my champion. I'm so grateful for your unwavering support, wise advice, and friendship.

Thank you to Chuck Hutchinson for tightening up the ship.

Thanks to Peter Turner for the sage advice.

Gratitude to Megan Lang for eagle eyes and "comma support." I can always count on you.

Love to Alexandra Franzen, my writing mentor, for inspiration on how to write and live well.

Deep appreciation for Rachel Pollack, Mary K. Greer, and Ruth Ann and Wald Amberstone. You opened the doors for Tarot folks.

Lots of love to my friends and family: My beloved children Megan and Nick, Jessica Schumacher, Simone Salmon, Tanya Geisler, Briana Saussy, Alexa Fischer, Danielle Cohen, Shaheen Miro, Elliot Eernisse, Suzi Dronzek, Heatherleigh Navarre, Chris Zydel, Jackie and Guy Dayen, Diane Bloom, Naha Armady, Pleasant Gehman, Lorri Davis, Damien Echols, Meg Jones Wall, Jeanna Kadlec, Mecca Woods, Mat Auryn, Courtney Weber, Hilary Parry Haggerty, Amy Zerner, Monte Farber, Arwen Lynch Poe, James Wells, Andrew McGregor, The Hierophant Writing Circle, and too many others to name. You know who you are.

Thanks to Mom and Dad, who taught me so much. Wish you were here to see all the books (and my grandson!).

Biggest gratitude to my life partner, soul mate, and best friend, Terry. My life is complete because of you. Let's have many more lifetimes together, deal?

And thank you to Holden, for giving me something to live for.

RESOURCES

Grief

AfterTalk: *www.aftertalk.com*

Camp Widow: *https://campwidow.org*

The Dougy Center for Grieving Children and Families: *www.dougy.org*

Fernside: Center for Grieving Children: *www.fernside.org*

The Grief Toolbox: *https://thegrieftoolbox.com*

Refuge in Grief: *https://refugeingrief.com*

Death

Association for Death Education and Counseling: *www.adec.org*

Hospice Foundation of America: *https://hospicefoundation.org*

Orphan Wisdom: *https://orphanwisdom.com*

Mental Health

Suicide Prevention Hotline: *https://988lifeline.org*

7 Cups: Free Online Counseling: *www.7cups.com*

I'm Alive: *www.imalive.org*

Youth Crisis Hotline: *1-800-448-4663*

Recommended Reading

Tarot

21 Ways to Read a Tarot Card by Mary K. Greer (Llewellyn Publications, 2006)

Seventy-Eight Degrees of Wisdom, Third Edition, Revised, by Rachel Pollack (Weiser Books, 2019)

Tarot Wisdom by Rachel Pollack (Llewellyn Publications, 2008)

Tarot for Troubled Times by Shaheen Miro and Theresa Reed (Weiser Books, 2019)

Tarot: No Questions Asked: Mastering the Art of Intuitive Reading by Theresa Reed (Weiser Books, 2020)

Choice Centered Tarot by Gail Fairfield (Weiser Books, 2000)

Tarot for the Healing Heart: Using Inner Wisdom to Heal Body and Mind by Christine Jette (Llewellyn Publications, 2001)

Grief

It's OK That You're Not OK, First Edition, by Megan Devine (Sounds True, 2017)

How to Carry What Can't Be Fixed by Megan Devine (Sounds True, 2021)

Finding Refuge: Heart Work for Healing Collective Grief by Michelle Cassandra Johnson (Shambhala, 2021)

Grief Is Love: Living with Loss by Marisa Renee Lee (Legacy Lit, 2022)

Dying

Die Wise by Stephen Jenkinson (North Atlantic Books, 2015)

Advice for Future Corpses (and Those Who Love Them): A Practical Perspective on Death and Dying, Reprint Edition, by Sally Tisdale (Gallery Books, 2019)

The Art of Dying Well: A Practical Guide to a Good End of Life, Reprint Edition, by Katy Butler (Scribner, 2020)

A Beginner's Guide to the End: Practical Advice for Living Life and Facing Death by Dr. BJ Miller and Shoshana Berger (Simon & Schuster, 2020)

Buddhism

Nothing Special, First Edition, by Charlotte Joko Beck (HarperOne, 1993)

How We Live Is How We Die by Pema Chödrön (Shambhala, 2022)

When Things Fall Apart: Heart Advice for Difficult Times, Anniversary Edition, by Pema Chödrön (Shambhala, 2016)

Yoga

Yoga for Grief and Loss, First Edition, by Karla Helbert (Singing Dragon, 2015)

The Chakras in Grief and Trauma, First Edition, by Karla Helbert (Singing Dragon, 2019)

Healing Through Yoga: Transform Loss into Empowerment—With More Than 75 Yoga Poses and Meditations by Paul Denniston (Chronicle Prism, 2022)

Trauma-Informed Yoga: A Toolbox for Therapists: 47 Practices to Calm, Balance, and Restore the Nervous System by Joanne Spence (PESI Publishing & Media, 2021)

About the Author

Theresa Reed (aka "The Tarot Lady") has worked as a full-time tarot card reader for thirty years. She is the author of *Twist Your Fate: Manifest Success with Astrology and Tarot*, *Tarot, No Questions Asked—Mastering the Art of Intuitive Reading*, *Astrology For Real Life (A No B.S. Guide for the Astro-Curious)*, *Tarot for Kids*, and *The Tarot Coloring Book*, an illustrated tour through the world of Tarot with coloring sheets for every card in the deck. Theresa is also the coauthor of *Tarot for Troubled Times* with Shaheen Miro.

In addition to writing, teaching, and speaking at tarot conferences, Theresa also runs a popular website—*TheTarotLady.com*—where she dishes out advice, inspiration, and tips for tarot lovers of all experience levels.

To Our Readers

Weiser Books, an imprint of Red Wheel/Weiser, publishes books across the entire spectrum of occult, esoteric, speculative, and New Age subjects. Our mission is to publish quality books that will make a difference in people's lives without advocating any one particular path or field of study. We value the integrity, originality, and depth of knowledge of our authors.

Our readers are our most important resource, and we appreciate your input, suggestions, and ideas about what you would like to see published.

Visit our website at *www.redwheelweiser.com*, where you can learn about our upcoming books and free downloads, and also find links to sign up for our newsletter and exclusive offers.

You can also contact us at *info@rwwbooks.com* or at

Red Wheel/Weiser, LLC
65 Parker Street, Suite 7
Newburyport, MA 01950